Contents

Chapter 2: Immigration and Economics

Immigration

Other Books of Related Interest:

At Issue Series

National Security

Current Controversies Series

Homeland Security

GLOBALVIEWPOINTS

Immigration

Tom Lansford, Book Editor

GREENHAVEN PRESS
A part of Gale, Cengage Learning

GALE
CENGAGE Learning

Detroit • New York • San Francisco • New Haven, Conn • Waterville, Maine • London

Christine Nasso, *Publisher*
Elizabeth Des Chenes, *Managing Editor*

© 2009 Greenhaven Press, a part of Gale, Cengage Learning

Gale and Greenhaven Press are registered trademarks used herein under license.

For more information, contact:
Greenhaven Press
27500 Drake Rd.
Farmington Hills, MI 48331-3535
Or you can visit our Internet site at gale.cengage.com

ALL RIGHTS RESERVED.
No part of this work covered by the copyright herein may be reproduced, transmitted, stored, or used in any form or by any means graphic, electronic, or mechanical, including but not limited to photocopying, recording, scanning, digitizing, taping, Web distribution, information networks, or information storage and retrieval systems, except as permitted under Section 107 or 108 of the 1976 United States Copyright Act, without the prior written permission of the publisher.

For product information and technology assistance, contact us at

Gale Customer Support, 1-800-877-4253
For permission to use material from this text or product, submit all requests online at www.cengage.com/permissions

Further permissions questions can be emailed to permissionrequest@cengage.com

Articles in Greenhaven Press anthologies are often edited for length to meet page requirements. In addition, original titles of these works are changed to clearly present the main thesis and to explicitly indicate the author's opinion. Every effort is made to ensure that Greenhaven Press accurately reflects the original intent of the authors. Every effort has been made to trace the owners of copyrighted material.

Cover image Mauro Seminara/AFP/Getty Images.

LIBRARY OF CONGRESS CATALOGING-IN-PUBLICATION DATA

Immigration / Tom Lansford, book editor.
    p. cm. -- (Global viewpoints)
    Includes bibliographical references and index.
    ISBN 978-0-7377-4158-2 (hardcover)
    ISBN 978-0-7377-4159-9 (pbk.)
    1. Emigration and immigration. 2. Citizenship. I. Lansford, Tom.
    JV6201.I454 2009
    304.8--dc22

                                                                    2008045079

Printed in the United States of America
    2 3 4 5 6   14 13 12 11 10
ED306

Chapter 3: Immigration and National Identity

Chapter 4: Immigration and National Security

Foreword

"*The problems of all of humanity can only be solved by all of humanity.*"
—*Swiss author Friedrich Dürrenmatt*

Global interdependence has become an undeniable reality. Mass media and technology have increased worldwide access to information and created a society of global citizens. Understanding and navigating this global community is a challenge, requiring a high degree of information literacy and a new level of learning sophistication.

Building on the success of its flagship series, *Opposing Viewpoints*, Greenhaven Press has created the *Global Viewpoints* series to examine a broad range of current, often controversial topics of worldwide importance from a variety of international perspectives. Providing students and other readers with the information they need to explore global connections and think critically about worldwide implications, each *Global Viewpoints* volume offers a panoramic view of a topic of widespread significance.

Drugs, famine, immigration—a broad, international treatment is essential to do justice to social, environmental, health, and political issues such as these. Junior high, high school, and early college students, as well as general readers, can all use *Global Viewpoints* anthologies to discern the complexities relating to each issue. Readers will be able to examine unique national perspectives while, at the same time, appreciating the interconnectedness that global priorities bring to all nations and cultures.

Material in each volume is selected from a diverse range of sources, including journals, magazines, newspapers, nonfiction books, speeches, government documents, pamphlets, organization newsletters, and position papers. *Global Viewpoints* is truly global, with material drawn primarily from international sources available in English and secondarily from U.S. sources with extensive international coverage.

Features of each volume in the *Global Viewpoints* series include:

- An **annotated table of contents** that provides a brief summary of each essay in the volume, including the name of the country or area covered in the essay.

- An **introduction** specific to the volume topic.

- A **world map** to help readers locate the countries or areas covered in the essays.

- For each viewpoint, an **introduction** that contains notes about the author and source of the viewpoint explains why material from the specific country is being presented, summarizes the main points of the viewpoint, and offers three **guided reading questions** to aid in understanding and comprehension.

- **For further discussion** questions that promote critical thinking by asking the reader to compare and contrast aspects of the viewpoints or draw conclusions about perspectives and arguments.

- A worldwide list of **organizations to contact** for readers seeking additional information.

- A **periodical bibliography** for each chapter and a **bibliography of books** on the volume topic to aid in further research.

- A comprehensive **subject index** to offer access to people, places, events, and subjects cited in the text, with the countries covered in the viewpoints highlighted.

Global Viewpoints is designed for a broad spectrum of readers who want to learn more about current events, history, political science, government, international relations, economics, environmental science, world cultures, and sociology—students doing research for class assignments or debates, teachers and faculty seeking to supplement course materials, and others wanting to understand current issues better. By presenting how people in various countries perceive the root causes, current consequences, and proposed solutions to worldwide challenges, *Global Viewpoints* volumes offer readers opportunities to enhance their global awareness and their knowledge of cultures worldwide.

Introduction

"You've had enough, haven't you? Enough of this rabble? Well, we're going to get rid of them for you."

—*Nicholas Sarkozy*

On October 27, 2005, in Clichy-sous-Bois, a suburb of Paris, France, police were called to investigate a possible burglary at a construction site. When they arrived, a group of ten nearby youths, all immigrants or children of immigrants, fled, believing that the police were after them. Three of the teenagers climbed a fence and tried to hide in a power station. All three were electrocuted. Two of the young men, Zyed Benna and Bouna Traore, were killed, while a third suffered massive injuries but survived. Tensions were already high following comments by then Minister of the Interior, Nicholas Sarkozy, who referred to unemployed youth in the urban ghettos as "rabble." The death of the two youths sparked a wave of protests and riots across France. Many immigrants in France from North Africa or other Muslim regions had faced a range of discrimination and racism for many years. Angry over high unemployment and alienation, they vented their rage in the streets.

After several nights of mob violence in the suburbs of Paris, by November 3, rioting had spread to all of France's largest cities. It ultimately affected more than 200 cities and towns. Rioters torched cars and businesses, and they even burned down a school and a Catholic church. On November 8, French President Jacques Chirac declared a national state of emergency and deployed an additional 18,000 police and security forces. However, the violence continued to spread. On November 12, arsonists disabled a power station, causing the power to go out in much of Amiens. The French Parliament approved a three-month extension of the state of emergency on November 16.

The government also undertook a number of other steps. Curfews were put in place and Sarkozy ordered the deportation of any non-citizens that were arrested for involvement in the rioting. The government announced that it was strengthening enforcement of current French law. Some right-wing French politicians went further and called for the revocation of citizenship for any of those arrested who were naturalized French citizens. Civic and religious groups endeavored to curtail the rioting. Major Muslim organizations issued calls for peace and denounced the violence.

Reaction to the riots became increasingly divided along political lines. Conservatives and anti-immigrant nationalist groups blamed the chaos on foreigners and immigrants. Sarkozy quickly emerged as one of the harshest critics of the rioters and demonstrators. Some media outlets and editorials called for the deportation of illegal migrants and new, stricter immigration policies. On the other hand, many liberal and left-wing politicians and officials noted that while the violence and destruction of property was unacceptable, there were a number of underlying factors that contributed to the rioting. French Prime Minister Dominique de Villepin called the violence "a crisis in France's cities," but declared that the government response would be "firm and fair." He promised the French people that the government would enact measures to lower unemployment within immigrant communities. In a televised interview, the prime minister also noted that "We must struggle against discrimination," and that "Everyone's behavior must change. . . . We must have a welcoming republic where everyone must be respected."

France is a country that prides itself on a generous social welfare system and political and social equality for all. However, many immigrants remain disproportionately poor and isolated from the rest of society. In France, a significant number of immigrants live in large urban areas in public housing projects. In 2005, the proportion of people who were foreign-born in French cities was 16 percent, while in the rest of France it was only 6 percent. Meanwhile, the unemployment rate of immigrants in France was 24 percent, more than twice the national unemployment rate of 10 percent. Among youths, the unemployment rate of immigrants or the children of immigrants was 40 percent, compared with 20 percent for natives. Immigrants often face discrimination in employment and housing. The rioting highlighted the frustration many immigrants and descendents of immigrants felt toward the French government and society in general. French soccer star Lilian Thuram, who immigrated as a youth, noted that "Violence never happens for no reason. You have to understand where the malaise comes from. Before talking about law and order, you have to talk about social justice." De Villepin adopted an increasingly moderate approach through the crisis. He declared that "Our collective responsibility is to make difficult areas the same sort of territory as others in the republic." Some asserted that Sarkozy's bellicose attitude through the rioting had added fuel to the fire and contributed to the expansion of rioting. However, many in France supported Sarkozy's hardline.

By the time the riots subsided at the end of November, at least 8,970 cars had been destroyed and 300 buildings damaged. The disorder resulted in more than $350 million in property damage. One person was killed and thousands injured, including 126 police officers and firefighters. Police arrested over 2,800 people. Meanwhile, Sarkozy emerged as the frontrunner among conservatives in the 2007 presidential election. Sarkozy went on to win the general election with 53.6 percent of the vote. Following his victory, rioting occurred in several French cities and more than 740 people were arrested after at least 1,000 cars were destroyed. In November

2007, a new, albeit less severe, round of rioting broke out in France after two youths of immigrant origins were killed in Villiers-le-Bel following a collision with a police car.

As in France, immigration is a major issue among many other nations around the world. Developed countries such as Canada, Great Britain, and the United States struggle to find appropriate immigration policies that promote economic development, but maintain national security. In many countries, increased concern over the potential for terrorism has led to reexaminations of immigration policy. In addition, many countries struggle over the proper method by which immigrants become citizens or acquire political or social rights.

Many thousands of migrants come from developing nations. They leave their homes seeking a new life and economic opportunity. Once in their adopted countries, they often provide substantial support for families or loved ones back home, contributing to the economies of their homelands. However, the newcomers often face discrimination and other hardships in their new countries.

As the world's population becomes increasingly mobile, the issue of immigration will only grow in importance. Migrants can provide substantial economic and social benefits to both their new and old home nations. They can also be the source of political or social strife, and they can contribute to alterations in the customs and traditions of their new counties. Many argue that nations should have open borders and allow people to move as they please. Others contend that nations need restrictive immigration policies for economic, social, and security reasons. The contributors in *Global Viewpoints: Immigration* examine the many international controversies that have emerged over immigration. The authors explore four main areas: immigration and citizenship; the economic impact of immigration; how immigration affects national identity; and the relationship between immigration and national security. As the riots in France demonstrate, immigration is likely to remain a contentious issue as people increasingly seek better lives in countries other than their own.

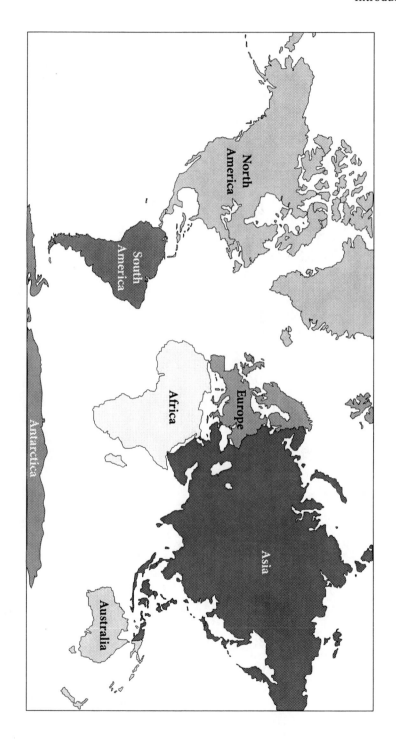

CHAPTER 1

Immigration and Citizenship

India Has Made Citizenship Allowances for Foreigners of Indian Origin

Poorvi Chothani

In the following viewpoint, the author describes the complicated nature of India's immigration laws. In 2006, India began allowing ethnic Indians who lived in other countries to register as overseas Indian citizens. This status gives these people the right to return and work in India, to enjoy economic, financial, and educational benefits; and, eventually, to gain full citizenship. Chothani is a lawyer who practices in both India and the United States, and is an expert on immigration law and intellectual property issues.

As you read, consider the following questions:

1. What Indian government agency controls immigration policies?
2. Who is eligible for person of Indian origin (PIO) status?
3. What benefits does an overseas citizen of India (OCI) receive in addition to those of a PIO?

Growing interest in doing business in India has resulted in an increasing number of foreigners travelling to India. Indian law does not place restrictions on the number of for-

Poorvi Chothani, "Navigating India's Immigration Law," *AsiaLaw*, April 2007, www.asialaw.com. Reproduced by permission.

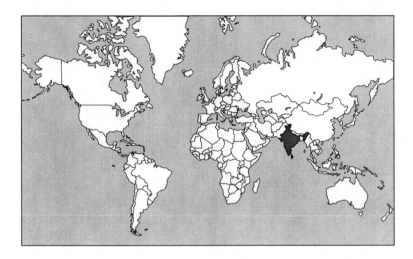

eign nationals that can work or do business in India, but the entry, stay and movements of foreign nationals in India are regulated by various Indian laws and rules passed by the Indian central government.

Policies and Procedures for Foreign Nationals

All foreign nationals planning to visit India should have a valid passport or other travel document and an appropriate visa [a form that grants permission to enter the country]. All passengers arriving in India are subject to immigration checks upon their arrival and departure from the country. There are no provisions for visas upon arrival. Those arriving in India without a visa bearing the correct validity dates and number of entries are subject to immediate deportation. Foreign nationals who have obtained Person of Indian Origin (PIO) cards or are registered as Overseas Citizens of India (OCI), which is granted to certain foreign nationals of Indian origin or their spouses, are exempt from certain visa requirements.

Visas can be obtained from the appropriate Indian embassy, high commission or consulate, depending on the location of residence. For instance, applicants who are citizens of

China may apply for Indian visas at the Indian embassy in Beijing. However, China citizens holding Hong Kong [identification] cards can apply for visas at the consulate in Hong Kong. The consulate at Hong Kong may issue visas to applicants who do not normally reside in the jurisdiction, after obtaining clearance from the India high commission in the applicant's country of residence.

A foreign national should apply for a visa depending on the category most suited to the purpose of the visit, which cannot be changed once the foreign national arrives in India. The consulate grants visas with validity from the date of issue and for the period requested by the applicant. There is a common visa application form for all categories of stay, which must be submitted with the prescribed visa fee and supporting documentation. Visa fees once received are not refunded, even if the application is withdrawn or the visa is denied.

The Indian Bureau of Immigration grants an applicant entry to India for a specific time, depending on the purpose of the visit. The changing of a visa status from one category to another is normally not allowed. The Ministry of Home Affairs has the power to convert visas in limited circumstances or extend visas within India.

A foreign national who can prove his or her Indian origin for up to three previous generations (or is the spouse of a citizen of India or a PIO), is eligible for a PIO card, which is valid for 15 years from the date of issue.

Most foreign nationals (including those of Indian origin) visiting India on a visa that permits a stay of more than 180 days must register with the Foreigners' Regional Registration Office (FRRO) with jurisdiction over the place in which the foreigner intends to stay within 14 days of his/her arrival.

In addition, some foreign nationals issued with visas which indicate that registration is required, irrespective of the duration of stay, should register with the appropriate FRRO within 14 days. A foreign national is required to appear in person before the appropriate registration officer with the relevant documentation. Nationals of certain countries are required to register within 24 hours to seven days of their arrival.

All foreign nationals are required to fill Form-C [for those visiting on Tourist Visas] under the Registration of Foreigners Rules when they stay in any hotel or commercial premises. It is the responsibility of the hotel owner to ensure that the foreign national complies with this requirement. This register has to be made available for inspection on demand by designated officials. Upon their departure, foreign nationals are required to provide information on the date and time of their departure and the address to which they are proceeding.

The Allowances for Persons of Indian Origin

A foreign national who can prove his or her Indian origin for up to three previous generations (or is the spouse of a citizen of India or a PIO), is eligible for a PIO card, which is valid for 15 years from the date of issue. Citizens of Pakistan, Bangladesh and other countries as specified by the central government are not eligible to receive these cards.

The PIO card gives the holder visa-free entry into India for 15 years and exemption from registration with an FRRO if the period of stay in India exceeds 180 days. In addition, PIO cardholders enjoy parity with non-resident Indians in economic, financial and educational fields. PIO cardholders can acquire, hold, transfer or dispose of immovable properties in India (except agricultural properties), open Indian rupee bank accounts, lend rupees to Indian residents and make investments in India. PIO cardholders' children can also obtain admission to educational institutions in India, on parity with non-resident Indians.

Illegal Indian Emigration to the U.S.

Turning stereotypes on their heads, a recent federal analysis of unauthorized immigration says the most rapidly growing source of illegal immigration is India, the same country whose engineers and programmers help power Google and other Silicon Valley companies, whose doctors heal the [California] Bay Area's sick, and whose entrepreneurs and venture capitalists have become a force on both sides of the international date line.

The U.S. Department of Homeland Security estimates that there are 270,000 unauthorized Indian natives in the United States, a 125 percent jump since 2000—the largest percentage increase of any nation with more than 100,000 illegal immigrants entering the United States.

Mike Swift,
"Indians Fastest-Growing Group of Bay Area's Illegal Immigrants,"
Oakland Tribune, *February, 19 2008.*

However, PIO cardholders cannot exercise any political rights, visit restricted/protected areas without permission, or undertake mountaineering, research and missionary work without additional permission. PIO cards are issued to eligible applicants through the Indian consulate in the country of their citizenship. Those staying in India on long-term visas may apply for it from the appropriate FRRO.

The Benefits for Overseas Citizens of India

As of January 2006, eligible foreign nationals can be registered as OCIs. Eligible foreign nationals include certain persons of Indian origin and individuals whose parents or grandparents migrated from India after January 26 1950, and their minor children. This is subject to the applicant being a citizen of a country which allows dual citizenship in some form or other. This provision is extended to such citizens of all countries other than those who have ever been citizens of Pakistan and Bangladesh.

Registration as an OCI is a one-time process that grants all the benefits that are available to PIO cardholders, with some additional benefits. These include a lifelong multi-entry and multi-purpose visa to visit, live or work in India, without travel restrictions within the country or the employment visa requirements that apply to PIOs. An OCI is not required to register with an FRRO for any length of stay in India.

An individual registered as an OCI for five years and who has lived in India for one year is eligible to gain full Indian citizenship. To avail of full Indian citizenship, a foreign national will have to relinquish his foreign nationality.

The Application Process

The OCI registration process is to be initiated online, at the Ministry of Home Affairs Web site, and completed by sending the supporting documents to the appropriate office. An application fee has to be submitted with the hard copy of the application. Individuals holding PIO cards may pay reduced fees.

An OCI certificate is issued to the applicant within a few weeks unless there are reports of criminal cases, in which case it could take longer. All applications are scrutinized by the Indian central government. The registration is subject to cancellation if it is found that it involved the aid of fraud, false representation or the concealment of any material facts.

Individuals wishing to obtain PIO cards should apply only in their country of citizenship. However, individuals can register as OCIs at the Indian commission or consulate in the country in which they reside or, in some instances, even while they are in India.

Indian nationals who have recently acquired nationality of another country are required to surrender their Indian passport to the consulate for cancellation at the time of applying for an Indian visa for the first time with their foreign passport.

A PIO cardholder who travels to India for a purpose other than a visit requires an appropriate visa. However, this does not apply to an OCI. Certain foreign nationals may acquire citizenship of India by naturalization if they have resided in India for the prescribed duration. Eligible OCIs may acquire Indian citizenship after staying in India for one year, provided that they have been registered as OCIs for five years.

Sweden Changed Its Citizenship Laws to Better Accommodate Immigrants

Per Gustafson

In the following viewpoint, the author explores the reasons why Sweden, in 2001, changed its laws to allow citizens of other countries to enjoy the rights and responsibilities of Swedish citizenship. Gustafson notes that Swedish law is based on the assumption that everyone living in the country should have the same political, legal, and economic rights. The Swedes also see dual citizenship as a means to better integrate people into the broader society. Gustafson is a scholar who earned his doctorate in sociology from Göteborg University in Sweden.

As you read, consider the following questions:

1. How long do immigrants have to wait before they can become Swedish citizens? What exceptions are made for immigrants from Nordic countries?

2. Before the citizenship law was changed in 2001, what exceptions were granted to allow dual citizenship?

3. According to the viewpoint, does dual citizenship reduce ethnic discrimination?

Per Gustafson, "Globalisation, Multiculturalism and Individualism: The Swedish Debate on Dual Citizenship," *Journal of Ethnic and Migration Studies*, vol. 28, no. 3, July 2002, pp. 467–72. Copyright © 2002 Taylor & Francis Ltd. Reproduced by permission of author and Taylor & Francis Ltd.

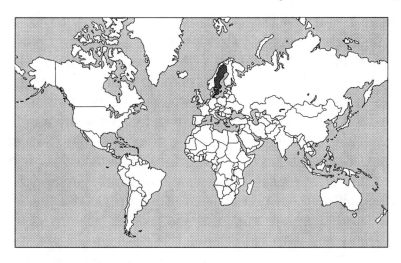

The policy on immigrants and integration pursued in Sweden since the mid-1970s explicitly accepts ethnic and cultural diversity. It states that all Swedish residents, regardless of ethnic/cultural background, should have equal rights and opportunities, as well as equal obligations and a common responsibility for the development of society. The policy is based on a 'cultural freedom of choice' with regard to cultural identity and assimilation. It also includes, among other things, public funding of numerous immigrant organisations, and local and regional voting rights for foreign residents. Swedish citizenship is available for immigrants after five years' residence (two years for immigrants from the Nordic countries), with no formal claims of cultural or linguistic assimilation.

Immigrants Face Limitations

However, this policy has not precluded ethnic cleavages in Swedish society. Since the early 1990s, immigrants (whether they are Swedish citizens or not) are substantially more affected by unemployment than the majority population, and also display low and decreasing rates of political participation. Several explanations for this development have been proposed—the changing character of immigration to Sweden (from labour migrants to refugees), new demands on the labour market, economic recession and the subsequent reduction of the public sector. . . . [T]he current integration policy does not enable immigrants to promote their collective interests in the political sphere. Firstly, the Swedish corporatist model is based on class, and has therefore left little room for immigrant organisations. Secondly, since the 1980s, Swedish integration policy has increasingly focused on individual rights and individual equality rather than on minority group rights. This policy . . . guarantees far-reaching formal equality, but has failed to achieve true social and political inclusion of immigrants in Sweden. In addition, the development described here has been accompanied by signs of increasing xenophobia in the Swedish population, and by more restrictive Swedish immigration policy.

. . . before July 2001, Swedish citizens who by their own choice became citizens of another state automatically lost their citizenship, and foreign nationals who opted for naturalisation in Sweden had to give up their former citizenship.

In spite of its relatively liberal policies on integration and naturalisation, Sweden has upheld a restrictive view of dual citizenship, just as most other northern European countries have. The previous Swedish citizenship law, which had been in force since 1951, did not in principle allow dual citizenship, and Sweden was one of the signatories of the 1963 European convention on reduction of cases of multiple nationality. Thus, before July 2001, Swedish citizens who by their own choice became citizens of another state automatically lost their Swedish citizenship, and foreign nationals who opted for naturalisation in Sweden had to give up their former citizenship. Dual citizenship was only approved in exceptional cases, the most important ones being children with parents of different nationalities, and immigrants eligible for naturalisation but whose former home countries refused to cancel their original citizenship.

Increased Dual Citizenship

Yet, with increasing international migration and, in particular, many refugees gaining Swedish citizenship without being released from their former citizenship, the number of dual citizens in Sweden has increased rapidly despite the restrictive legislation. In the mid-1980s, 100,000 Swedish citizens living in Sweden were said to be citizens of another state too, whereas the 1997 citizenship commission estimated the number of dual citizens in Sweden as around 300,000—100,000 being dual citizens by birth and almost 200,000 through naturalisation or formal registration (the latter procedure applying to children and youth in certain cases). No estimates seem to have been made about the number of Swedes with dual citizenship living abroad. In addition, many foreign citizens live in Sweden as legal residents without acquiring Swedish citizenship (over 500,000 in 1997). This has for some time been considered problematic with regard to integration and political participation.

Already in the 1980s a parliamentary commission considered the possibility of facilitating immigrants' integration into Swedish society by means of more liberal legislation on dual citizenship. No such measures were taken at that time, mainly because Sweden was not prepared to withdraw its ratification of the 1963 European convention. The commission also pointed out security issues and dual voting rights as possible, although minor, problematic consequences of dual citizenship. There was nevertheless a strong desire to promote dual citizenship. A government bill based on the work of the commission did in fact suggest, firstly, a liberalisation of existing, naturalisation practice with regard to dual citizenship, and secondly, that Sweden should work, preferably together with the other Nordic countries, for increased international acceptance of dual citizenship and ultimately a revision of the 1963 European convention. However, after a change of government in 1991 (from a Social Democratic one to a centre-right coalition) this bill was withdrawn.

Revising the Citizenship Legislation

In 1997, a new parliamentary commission was appointed to make a general review of Swedish citizenship legislation and, in an additional directive, to 'analyse and consider the consequences of a general abandonment of the present principle that dual citizenship should be avoided, and suggest any constitutional and other measures which may result from these considerations'. The commission presented its final report in March 1999, suggesting a new citizenship law that fully accepted dual citizenship. After an extensive consultative procedure, a government bill was presented to Parliament in June 2000, closely following the citizenship commission's report with regard to the arguments in favour of dual citizenship as well as to the proposed new legislation. The new law was passed by Parliament in February 2001, and came into force in July the same year. Thus, foreign nationals who acquire Swedish citizenship through naturalisation no longer have to renounce their former citizenship, and Swedes who acquire the citizenship of another state may also remain Swedish citizens. In addition, those who have lost their Swedish citizenship because of the old legislation may regain it if they make an application within two years. In all cases, this of course requires that the other state in question also accepts dual citizenship; moreover, the Swedish law will not apply until July 2002 in relation to other signatories of the 1963 European convention. Sweden has now denounced this convention, and instead ratified the 1997 European convention on citizenship, which is neutral with regard to dual citizenship.

Sweden's Citizenship Law

On 1 July 2001 Sweden acquired a new Citizenship Act. Among other things, the Act means that dual citizenship is possible. Thus, anyone acquiring Swedish citizenship can keep his/her previous citizenship if the law of that country so permits. Swedish citizens who acquire another citizenship can also keep their Swedish citizenship if the other country's laws so permit. The new law makes it easier for children and young people to become Swedish citizens.

Government Offices of Sweden,
"Swedish Citizenship," April 25, 2004. www.sweden.gov.se.

When the new law was adopted, only the Moderate Party (liberal/conservative, with 23 percent of the votes in Parliament) voted against it. In the public debate about the commission's report and the proposed new legislation, some newspapers (right-of-centre), some public authorities (including the Armed Forces and the Aliens Appeals Board) and several individuals also more or less forcefully opposed dual citizenship. However, most participants in the debate were in favour, and an opinion poll made in March 1999, when the commission's report was presented, indicated that dual citizenship was accepted by a narrow majority of the Swedish population.

The Modernisation of Swedish Legislation

A common starting-point for those in favour of dual citizenship was to argue that contemporary society was characterised by globalisation or internationalisation, and by increasing international migration. In consequence, it was suggested, firstly, that Sweden was becoming an increasingly multiethnic or multicultural society and, secondly, that individuals often developed strong and durable ties to several different countries. A Social Democratic [Party] editorial illustrates these claims:

> Since World War II a new world has evolved. Technology, economy and communications have made us more mobile. More and more people leave Sweden and settle abroad, to study or to work, for longer or shorter periods of time. Others move in the other direction—to Sweden. Almost one million residents in Sweden today have foreign backgrounds. We are living in a multicultural society, where notions of nationality, citizenship and identity are changing.

This situation, it was argued, differed substantially from the conditions under which the earlier citizenship law was worked out. The principle of not accepting dual citizenship was already undermined as a large number of dual citizens were indeed living in Sweden, and without causing any serious problems. There was also an international trend towards increasing acceptance, manifested, for example, in a new European convention that opened up for dual citizenship. Thus, the proposed acceptance of dual citizenship was described as a necessary 'modernisation' of the old citizenship legislation, in order to adapt it to a new national and international situation. This emerges as a first important reason for the acceptance of dual citizenship.

More specifically, claims about a multicultural society pointed towards the need to manage ethnic/cultural diversity within Sweden, to promote the integration of immigrants and to reduce problems of social exclusion. Claims about dual or multiple national bonds, on the other hand, pointed towards an individual perspective, focusing on the experiences and desires of migrants—on identity and on individual freedom of choice with regard to citizenship and national belonging. From both these perspectives, the proponents advocated a more liberal stance towards dual citizenship. . . .

Some Want to Maintain the Nation-State Order

The opponents of dual citizenship, for their part, made few references to globalisation, and when they did, they de-emphasised its importance with regard to citizenship. National citizenship, the Moderate Party argued, should still be a matter of undivided national allegiance:

> The Moderate Party attaches great importance to citizenship, and this importance is not in any way reduced by the general globalisation or by [Sweden's] membership in the European Union. We are certainly not witnessing the end of the nation-state. Citizenship gives the individual clear and unequivocal rights and obligations in relation to the state. The loyalty to the country where one is a citizen should be absolute.

Thus, in the debate about dual citizenship, processes of internationalisation and globalisation were put in opposition to the nation-state order discussed above—that of autonomous and homogenous nation-states and unique national belonging manifested by national citizenship. It was generally assumed that the old citizenship law reflected (and to some extent served to maintain) such a nation-state order. Most opponents of dual citizenship wanted to uphold this order and based their arguments almost exclusively on a national perspective. The proponents of dual citizenship, on the other hand, claimed that the citizenship legislation needed revision in order to accommodate the new situation brought about by globalisation and increasing international mobility. Some of the proponents welcomed this development, whereas others accepted dual citizenship with much hesitation, as a regrettable but necessary adaptation. In either case, however, the arguments of the proponents were not based solely on a national perspective (although that perspective was present in their accounts too), but also used, on the one hand, a global or international perspective and, on the other hand, a more individualistic perspective.

Both sides agreed that the integration of immigrants in Swedish society was something which was highly desirable.

Political Participation and Integration

Problems of social exclusion and decreasing political participation among immigrants have been much discussed and deplored in the public debate in Sweden, and arguments about integration and participation were also important in the discussions about dual citizenship. Opponents as well as proponents usually employed a national perspective in these arguments, and regarded the integration of immigrants as a matter of ensuring social cohesion and the legitimacy of national political institutions.

Both sides agreed that the integration of immigrants in Swedish society was something which was highly desirable, but it was debated whether or not the acceptance of dual citizenship would facilitate integration. The commission's report had in fact relatively little to say about integration; yet politicians, authorities and editorial writers, and often also immigrants and their organisations, frequently argued that acceptance of dual citizenship would encourage immigrants to naturalise and thus gain the right to vote and to participate fully in Swedish political life. The acquisition of Swedish citizenship was thus regarded as an important step towards integration:

> The National Integration Office considers the proposal about dual citizenship to be favourable for integration. It opens up new opportunities for many immigrants to feel that they are

part of Swedish society, and hopefully also to gain the sense of responsibility with regard to societal obligations that follows from fully equal rights.

Some proponents also argued that Swedish citizenship might help to reduce ethnic discrimination, for example, on the labour market; others suggested that dual citizenship would be a symbolic manifestation that immigrants could become fully accepted members of Swedish society without having to deny their origins. This latter argument also points towards an individual perspective, focusing on emotional and identity issues. . . .

Russia Struggles to Balance the Need for New Citizens with Domestic Opposition to Immigrants

Zygmunt Dzieciolowski

In the following viewpoint, the author asserts that the rising age of the population in Russia and the nation's low birth rate have created a critical need for new immigrants to be workers. However, Dzieciolowski points out that many people in Russia oppose immigration and those who are in the country illegally are sometimes subject to brutal repression and violence. Consequently, Russia has to develop a new immigration policy that balances its needs for workers with public sentiment against immigrants. Dzieciolowski is a Polish journalist and the author of Planet Russia, *published in 1985.*

As you read, consider the following questions:

1. How much do employers in Russia have to pay in fines if they are caught employing illegal workers?
2. Workers from what country helped modernize the infrastructure of the province of Chukotka?
3. According to the viewpoint, how much money is sent from Russia to neighboring countries each year by immigrants?

Zygmunt Dzieciolowski, "Russia's Immigration Challenge," *Open Democracy*, June 15, 2007. www.opendemocracy.net. Reproduced by permission.

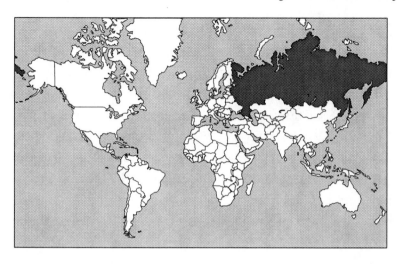

For the last three years [since 2004] Mansur Mirzayev, a 22-year-old Uzbek, has been living in Moscow. He came to the Russian capital from the poverty-stricken province of Andijan—which was, after his departure, the scene of a notorious massacre by the state forces of Islam Karimov [President of Uzbekistan] in May 2005. No jobs were available there in the region of Uzbekistan close to the border with Kyrgyzstan, so together with a number of local people Mansur decided to take the risk of moving to Russia.

On arrival, he had a bit of luck: one of his friends recommended him for a job as loader at the market in the district of Zhulebino, to the east of Moscow. It was simple, menial work, requiring Mansur to carry heavy loads of goods on his rusty trolley for the entire day. In the beginning he worked "black" [illegally], as securing proper documents was next to impossible; but militia who kept an eye on the market were easy to bribe. Each side knew the rules of the game. The militia understood that charging Uzbeks and Tajiks too high a sum would mean they would seek jobs elsewhere; and their victims did not object paying as it guaranteed a minimum of safety when their papers and registration were not in order.

New Laws Endanger Immigrant Workers

Things changed when the Russian government introduced new registration and immigration laws which came into force in January and April 2007. Now Mansur and his friends were in a tight situation; their employer would risk a fine of up to $30,000 if he gave them jobs without proper Moscow registration and work permits. They had no choice but to pay out again—this time a lump sum in bribes to the officials processing their applications. From that point, however, they felt freed from their obligation to pay their regular fee to the militia.

Nothing angers market-cops more than losing their regular source of income. A few weeks ago, they arrested Mansur and some of his colleagues on trumped-up charges and took them to the local militia station.

There, the arrested Uzbeks were forced onto their knees. According to witnesses, one of the four militiamen taking part in the interrogation seemed to be drunk, and his uniform differed from those of regular servicemen. In an instant of anger, he pulled out his gun and shot Mansur, who missed death because the bullet only wounded the side of his neck. The Uzbek man survived and was taken to the nearest hospital.

Meanwhile, those of Mansur's colleagues from the market who had escaped the dragnet raised the alarm among Moscow's human-rights activists. When a few of those activists arrived at the Zhulebino militia station, they discovered that after the shooting Mansur's arrested mates (even those whose spoken Russian was extremely poor) were being pressed by their captors into testifying that the wounded man had been behaving violently and carried all responsibility for the incident. In the end it became evident that the contretemps was all about money and the militia's demand for bribes even from those migrant workers whose papers were in order.

Russia's Falling Population

The World Bank estimates that the number of Russians could decline from 143 million to 100 million within the next half-century, a trend line that if extended to its logical, if highly unlikely, end point, would see the Russians die out within five generations. The population has already dropped between 700,000 and 750,000 a year in the past decade, and the pace is accelerating with Russia's unique mix of low birth rates, plunging life expectancy and low immigration.

Graeme Smith, "Russia Shrinks,"
Globe and Mail, *April 21, 2006. www.theglobeandmail.com.*

Immigrants Attempt to Settle in Their New Home

The Zhulebino incident illustrates all too well the dangers faced by migrant workers who come to Russia. Most are fleeing extreme poverty in their own countries (usually the post-Soviet republics), are poorly educated, unable to communicate in fluent Russian, and thus forced to adapt to a corrupt Russian legal system when refusal to play by the "informal" rules could cost them dearly. A few who are especially enterprising or energetic—or simply desperate for work—might travel outside the old Soviet space, sometimes as far as South Korea. Most have no choice.

Russia's current booming economy, fuelled by high prices for oil, gas and metals, needs these workers badly. Without an army of low-qualified, unskilled workers, some sectors of the Russian economy—construction, municipal and domestic services, the retail trade—would suffer severely, if not be altogether paralysed. Without the dark-haired Tajik immigrant workers, there would be nobody to sweep the Moscow streets and fix their holes, or build the high-rise modern office buildings and suburban dachas going up all over Moscow.

The Tajiks alone are not numerous enough. Russian companies short of labour are seeking to bring workers even from China and Turkey. In the far-eastern city of Blagoveshchensk, as early as the late 1990s, I saw Chinese workers renovating the local railway station and growing vegetables in otherwise bankrupt Russian collective farms. More recently, 2,000 Turkish *gastarbeiter* [guest workers] have helped Roman Abramovich, governor of Chukotka and Russia's richest oligarch [one of a few people who control the nation's government], to modernise the infrastructure of his remote Arctic region.

In central Asia's poorest nations such as Tajikistan and Uzbekistan, recruiting workers for the Russian labour market is a murky business. The dealers penetrate most of the remote villages, promising fabulous wages and organising transport. In some regions during the Russian construction season, most of the men would embark on what might be a week-long bus journey to a far Russian location, leaving children and women behind. The cost of the trip goes up with every militia document-check on the way—and in order to avoid trouble, paying bribes is from the start a must.

When they arrive at their destination, the workers' accommodation would be most often overcrowded, crumbling, dirty, and lacking basic comforts. The recruiters would hold onto their passports and impose on them an extra charge of up to 50 percent of their earnings for "services" rendered. Such services would include helping to release workers from the police station in the event of an experience like Mansur Mirzayev's.

Sometimes things happen the other way round, as for example when an immigrant worker from Kyrgyzstan shot a Russian flower-shop owner in a Moscow neighbourhood. Even some prominent representatives of the Kyrgyz community in Russia expressed concern over their compatriots' behaviour, arguing that their heavy drinking, unruliness, lack of language skills and ignorance of local Russian habits only increase the chance of conflict. Kyrgyzstan's former prime minister who now lives in Russia, Apas Jumagulov, was one of those who appealed to his fellow countrymen to make efforts to avoid tension with their new Russian neighbours.

Illegal workers (who do not pay taxes) cost the federal budget around $7 billion per year.

An Uncertain Immigrant Population

There are no reliable statistics in Russia concerning immigrant workers. Local tabloids publish alarming estimates that they number as many as 20 million (if true this would mean that a massive invasion of Russia by foreign nationals is effectively underway). Government officials, meanwhile, say that illegal workers (who do not pay taxes) cost the federal budget around $7 billion per year; on the other side, at approximately $10 billion per year, immigrant workers' transfer of funds to Tajikistan, Moldova, Uzbekistan, Kyrgyzstan, Georgia, and Azerbaijan make up a considerable proportion of these countries' national income.

Rostislav Kapelushnikov of the Moscow high school of economics counsels caution about frequently cited estimates of the number of foreign workers in the Russian Federation. A population of 142 million means that the number of people active in the labour market is not higher than 69 million. Kapelushnikov concludes there is no evidence whatsoever that the figure of 20 million foreign workers often quoted by the Russian media is correct; his own judgment is that foreign workers make up no more than 5 percent of the Russian labour market, with no more than 4 million in total.

Large industrial companies which also need unskilled workers try to avoid hiring foreigners; they would risk heavy fines employing them without proper permits, and securing these would be from their point of view both too costly and a time-consuming hassle. It is different for smaller independent businesses, which are difficult for the government to control. That is why migrant labour is concentrated in a few specific and highly visible areas such as construction. Perhaps that contributes to the widespread impression among Russians that foreign workers are "everywhere", and taking jobs away from the natives.

Russia's Population Crisis

In an interview with the www.cato.ru Web site, Rostislav Kapelushnikov maintains that Russia's demographic situation—the population is predicted to fall by 30 percent by 2050—means that a high demand for unskilled migrant labour will continue. Although their number is smaller than generally believed, Kapelushnikov agrees that only well formulated and efficiently implemented government policy can address the very serious problems usually connected with mass labour migration. Xenophobic feelings [fear of foreigners] are already high among the Russian population, and a lack of consistent policy may only reinforce them.

Russia may not be immune from the kind of problems that France has experienced with angry young immigrants and riots. But it would be even more dangerous and counterproductive, says Kapelushnikov, for the country to listen to those who call for a total ban on immigrant labour. Such a decision would only strengthen Russia's demographic crisis. One way or another, Russians are going to have to learn how to live alongside Mansur Mirzayev and millions like him.

Germany May Require a Test of Loyalty to Obtain Citizenship

Turkish Daily News

In the following viewpoint, a controversial citizenship test used by one German state is examined. The test was designed to ensure that immigrants, especially Muslim applicants, understand the basic political ideals and values of Germany. It is also designed to prevent individuals from becoming citizens who hold radical views that support political violence and that run counter to the German mainstream. The Turkish Daily News *is one of the largest English-language news outlets in Turkey.*

As you read, consider the following questions:

1. Applicants from how many countries are required to take the citizenship test in Baden-Wurttemberg?
2. According to the viewpoint, what are some of the topics on the controversial citizenship exam?
3. What group developed the "conscience test," an alternative to the citizenship test?

A proposal submitted by the Union 90/Greens Party in Germany for abolition of a "conscience test" for Muslim applicants for citizenship was turned down after intense debates in the German Federal Parliament last week.

Turkish Daily News, "Germany Debates Controversial Citizenship Loyalty Test for Muslims," January 22, 2006. Reproduced by permission.

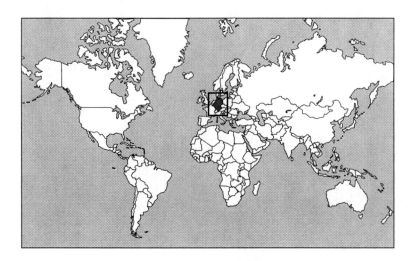

Debates Ensue over the Loyalty Test

Believed to be the first test of its kind in Europe, the southern state of Baden-Wurttemberg has created a two-hour oral exam to test the loyalty of immigrants, especially Muslims, towards Germany, its constitution and societal values. The practice has been in effect since Jan. 1, 2006.

Applicants for citizenship are required to answer 30 challenging questions and will have the right to become German citizens when they give "correct answers" to the questions.

Muslim applicants from 57 countries, including Turkey, are required to give correct answers to the questions in the 30-question test, which is assumed to prove that applicants think similar to the German Constitution. The applicants are required to state their opinion on the idea of democracy, political parties, and religious freedom. They are also asked to state what they would do upon learning about a terrorist operation under way and their reaction in the face of criticism leveled at a religion.

Baden-Wurttemberg is the only state nationwide to support the controversial test for Muslims seeking German citizenship.

Seeking the end of the practice, the parliamentary group of the Union 90/Greens Party opened the issue up to debate in the Federal Parliament but, after long debates, the proposal to annul the test was rejected with the votes of Free Democratic Party (FDP) and some Social Democratic Party (SDP) deputies.

During a speech in Parliament on Thursday, Baden-Wurttemberg Interior Minister Heribert Rech, from major coalition partner the Christian Democratic Union (CDU), deflected criticism of the practice and said, with the "conscience test" they did not discriminate against Muslims but wanted to determine the loyalty to the constitution and the country's democratic order of foreigners seeking German citizenship.

Ekin Deligöz, a deputy of Turkish origin from the Union 90/Greens Party, said there were also German citizens who didn't abide by the constitution.

"The presence of Germans who are enemies of the constitution is not a reason for the application of this test to foreigners," Rech said in response.

The Test's Arguable Effectiveness

The test questions, which were formulated by a special commission, range in topic from gender equality to homosexuality, honor killings and Western attire for young women and are expected to trigger discussion between applicants and officials.

"Although you may not want to believe it, there are intellectual Muslims in Germany. There are Germans who are against homosexuality or the democratic order. Instead of being engaged in discrimination, seek ways on how to shape society," Deligöz told the state interior minister.

Establishing an Immigrant Population in Germany

The majority [of Germany's immigrants] were invited to the country as *gastarbeiters,* or guest workers, mainly from Turkey. Faced with a labor shortage in the 1950s, and 60s, then-West Germany encouraged foreigners to fill positions in factories and in construction. . . .

Given temporary visas, the Germans expected the workers to come, make money and then head home.

What the government didn't count on was the employers' reluctance to let trained workers leave. So the men stayed and then brought their families—along with their traditions, religion and culture.

Rachel Elbaum, "Integration Questions Stir Passions,"
MSNBC, May 25 2006, www.msnbc.msn.com.

However, Rech said every individual should assume some responsibilities and that loyalty to the constitution and democratic rules top these responsibilities.

Rech emphasized that most of the Muslims abided by the law and easily became German citizens but warned that there were still radical movements.

Drawing attention to remarks made by some supporters of Islamic extremist Metin Kaplan during their testimony at a court after attaining German citizenship, Rech said the supporters stressed at the time that they were not loyal to the German Constitution and that only the rules of Shariah were valid for them.

Kaplan lived in Cologne until he was extradited to Turkey in October 2004. He leads a group, the Caliphate State, that calls for the replacement of Turkey's secular government with an Islamic state. His organization, which is outlawed in Turkey, was also banned in Germany in 2001 under legislation passed in the wake of the September 11 [2001] terrorist attacks in the United States to crack down on Islamist extremists.

"What we only want to see is the approval of our constitutional order," Rech said.

The Test May Discriminate

The Left Party deputy, Sevim Dağdelen, said the "conscience test" paved the way for prejudice against Muslims.

"This test is discriminating and degrades Muslims. Some questions in the test violate the relevant articles of the constitution on equality and privacy," she said.

Dağdelen claimed that ruling party officials in the southern German state were administering such a test to score their political objectives for the upcoming state elections.

One of the key questions in the test intends to find out Muslims' views about the September 11 attacks in the United States and March 2004 attacks in Madrid.

Addressing the state officials who imposed the test, Dağdelen said: "By behaving in this way, you harm both democracy and living together. The number of those who attain German citizenship in the state is decreasing. You do not encourage harmonization with this test. Give up this discriminatory practice."

Greens Party deputy Joseph Philip was among anti-conscience test deputies in Germany. He also said the test was discriminatory and the practice would not help weed out people in favor of violence.

SDP deputy Michael Buersch raised concerns over the practice of such a test for Muslims and emphasized that many Germans also could give "unexpected answers" to questions in the test.

FDP deputy Hartfrid Wolff said the practice was necessary but admitted that some questions were discriminatory.

One of the key questions in the test intends to find out Muslims' views about the September 11 attacks in the United States and March 2004 attacks in Madrid. "Were Jews responsible for the attacks? Were the ones who carried out the attacks terrorists or freedom fighters?" asks the test.

A Revision May Be in Order

The German-Turkish Forum told the German Christian Democratic Union Party that they had drafted an alternative test to be applied instead of the "conscience test" for those applicants who want to become German citizens.

Bülent Arslan, head of the forum, leveled criticism at the "conscience test" and said the test was asking people's opinions and it was not possible to make an assessment about citizenship on the basis of their personal opinions.

"We're in favor of a test asking applicants information about Germany," he added, noting that they would introduce a new test in the coming days.

Meanwhile, there are efforts to spread the loyalty test to other states in Germany.

Volker Bouffier, interior minister of Hessen state in Germany, said in a televised speech that they would administer a similar test for foreigners seeking citizenship.

He said the people living in the state should know and adopt the basics of the German Constitution.

Bouffier said the test would be applied to all foreigners, including Muslims. He said the aim of the test was not to root out terror suspects as it was the duty of departments in charge to protect the constitution.

The United States Needs to Improve the Processes That Allow Immigrants to Become Citizens

Souheila Al-Jadda

In the following viewpoint, the author uses the case of one Palestinian family to highlight the problems with the current U.S. immigration system. Flaws in the system through which people become U.S. citizens have resulted in lengthy delays for individuals and families who are trying to complete the process. The viewpoint also highlights several reform efforts that have been implemented within the government or proposed in Congress. Al-Jadda is a journalist and the associate producer of the program "Mosaic: News from the Middle East."

As you read, consider the following questions:

1. How many Palestinian refugees does the viewpoint identify worldwide?
2. How many FBI name-check investigation cases remained as of 2007?
3. According to Al-Jadda, what did the Department of Homeland Security take in 2005 to reduce the backlog of immigration cases?

Souheila Al-Jadda, "One Family's Nightmare," *USA Today*, September 26, 2007, p. 11A. Copyright © 2007, *USA Today*. Reproduced by permission.

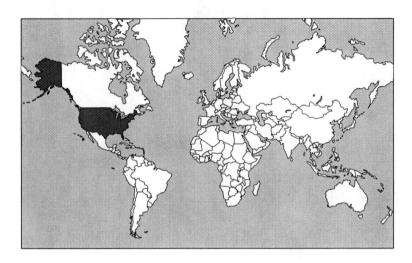

The Garadah family story is about how an American dream turned into an immigration nightmare. In 1998, Bassam Garadah and his wife, Maha Dakar, both Palestinians, applied for political asylum in the United States. In the ensuing nine years, the couple made a good life, raising four daughters born in America, all now younger than ten.

Earlier [in 2007], after a decade-long process of court hearings and appeals, the 6th Circuit Court of Appeals came back with a final decision on their asylum petition: denied. The family was left scrambling about what to do next.

... little attention has been paid to the law-abiding immigrants whose families have suffered through long delays and even errors because of backlogs at the U.S. Citizen and Immigration Services.

The Garadahs Are Disappointed by Immigration Services

The nation's immigration debate has been largely about the 12 million illegal immigrants in this country. But little attention has been paid to the law-abiding immigrants whose families have suffered through long delays and even errors because of backlogs at the U.S. Citizenship and Immigration Services (USCIS) and FBI.

So now Maha Dakar is being threatened with deportation—which would mean the family will likely be split apart. Several years ago, the couple tried to improve their odds by also applying for residency through their immediate relatives in the United States. But their applications will take at least five years—well beyond Maha's deportation deadline.

Their situation becomes more complicated by the family's background. Maha is a Jordanian citizen of Palestinian descent. She will likely be deported to Jordan. Bassam, who carries only Egyptian travel documents, has been refused entry to both Egypt and Jordan. The couple lived in Bulgaria and Kuwait before immigrating to the United States. But Kuwait will not allow the entire family to return because they are Palestinians and do not have citizenship rights. (In fact, the judge, in rejecting their asylum request, mistakenly ruled that they could return to Kuwait without facing persecution.)

Aside from reflecting the poor state of U.S. immigration services, the Garadah story also highlights how stateless and displaced Palestinian refugees, who number more than 4 million, are often mistreated in host countries. These refugees often are treated as second-class citizens. For those reasons and others, the Garadah family felt privileged to live in America.

As of September 2006, about 1.2 million immigration applicants had yet to be processed.

From Bad to Worse

On July 30, [2007] Rep. Steve Chabot, R-Ohio, introduced a bill that would allow Maha to remain in the United States while her immigration application is being considered. Chabot has been strongly opposed to illegal immigration, but he has said that Garadah family members entered the country legally, have broken no laws and should be allowed to stay given that their daughters are U.S. citizens. After Chabot's bill was introduced, USCIS decided not to enforce Maha's deportation until March 2009. Still, such bills are usually symbolic and have rarely passed. When they do pass, only an individual or family is helped. For families like the Garadahs, the path to legal immigration does not appear to be getting shorter:

- *Application backlog.* As of September 2006, about 1.2 million immigration applications had yet to be processed, USCIS reported then. Recently, however, USCIS ombudsman [investigates complaints against government entities] Prakash Khatri issued a report estimating that the backlog is more like 2.5 million cases—and rising. Some immigrants, he found, have been waiting many years for a decision to be made on their green card or citizenship applications.

- *FBI background checks.* After September 11 [2001], President [George W.] Bush folded Immigration and Naturalization Services into the new Department of Homeland Security, linking the immigration process with security policy. As a result, the FBI conducts name checks on all immigrant applications to screen for threats. According to the USCIS ombudsman report, FBI name checks "may be the single biggest obstacle to the timely . . . delivery of immigration benefits."

As of May [2007], 329,160 FBI name-check cases were pending. That's up nearly 40 percent from the previous year. USCIS does not include these cases in its own backlog estimates.

Problems with the System

Delayed applications can make the daily lives of these immigrants quite difficult.

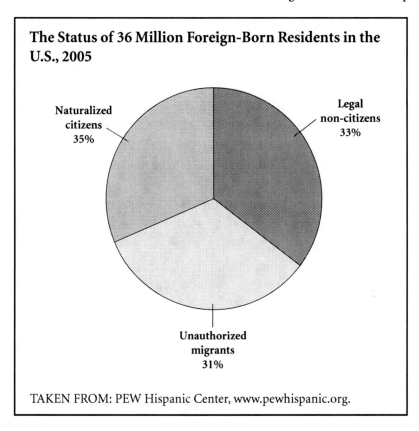

The Status of 36 Million Foreign-Born Residents in the U.S., 2005

Naturalized citizens 35%

Legal non-citizens 33%

Unauthorized migrants 31%

TAKEN FROM: PEW Hispanic Center, www.pewhispanic.org.

The Garadah family has not traveled outside the United States in the past ten years out of fear of being refused re-entry. Maha and Bassam also must apply for a work permit every year, making it difficult to hold down a job because their authorization papers often arrive months late, or sometimes not at all. Applicants often face difficulties obtaining driver's licenses, opening bank accounts and establishing a credit history to buy a home or car.

The fact that immigrants are willing to wait out the seemingly interminable immigration process shows the value that they place in living in the United States. Yet how does the nation reward them for trying the legal path? It allows their applications to become entangled in a bureaucracy that will ultimately fail many of them.

In 2005, Homeland Security tried to resolve the backlog by raising citizenship application fees to cover the cost of hiring more staff to process cases more quickly. Clearly, this has not worked. Fees were raised again [in] summer [2007], yet millions of applications are pending.

Comprehensive immigration reform in Congress [in 2007] appears dead. Perhaps an incremental approach would be more politically viable. Lawmakers could first concentrate their efforts on correcting the glitches in the system that affect legal immigration, before turning to illegal immigration. After all, if the legal process was more efficient and less daunting, perhaps the illegal immigration problems wouldn't be quite so bad.

USCIS aims to serve legal immigrants, and its motto is "Securing America's promise."

For the Garadah family and many others, that promise is being broken.

Periodical Bibliography

The following articles have been selected to supplement the diverse views presented in this chapter.

Karen Juanita Carrillio "Immigrant Rights Movement Affecting African Americans," *New York Amsterdam News*, April 6, 2006.

Jane Freedman "Citizenship, Borders and Identity in an Enlarging EU," *Parliamentary Affairs*, October 2006.

Simon Green "Immigration, Asylum, and Citizenship in Germany: The Impact of Unification and the Berlin Republic," *West European Politics*, October 1, 2001.

Christian Joppke "Comparative Citizenship: A Restrictive Turn in Europe?" *Law & Ethics of Human Rights*, July 2008.

Riva Kastoryano "Contested Citizenship," *Ethnicities*, March 2008.

Sabita Majid "Between Here and There," *Maclean's*, January 10, 2005.

Maurice Maschino "Are You Sure You're French?" *Le Monde Diplomatique*, June 2002.

Georges Nzongola-Ntalaja "Citizenship, Political Violence and Democratization in Africa," *Global Governance*, October 2004.

Ramesh Ponnuru "Born in the USA: Should that Automatically Make You a Citizen?" *National Review*, February 27, 2006.

Carlota Sole "Immigration Policies in Southern Europe," *Journal of Ethnic and Migration Studies*, November 2004.

GLOBALVIEWPOINTS

CHAPTER 2

Immigration and Economics

Ireland's Economic Growth Has Reversed Centuries of Outward Migration

Piaras MacÉinrí and Paddy Walley

In the following viewpoint, the authors analyze immigration to Ireland. The viewpoint examines the historic reversal that occurred in the late 1990s when Ireland went from a continual loss of its citizens due to emigration to a net gain thanks to immigration. Improvements in the economy were key to this reversal as more people moved to Ireland to take advantage of the country's growing economy. Piaras MacÉinrí is a lecturer in geography at the University College Cork, and Paddy Walley is an author and consultant.

As you read, consider the following questions:

1. By the late 1990s, what was the unemployment rate in Ireland?
2. Which is the only country in Europe with a higher immigration rate than Ireland?
3. In the last census, what percentage of the population declared themselves to be Irish?

Ireland's history has been one of constant emigration. Even in the very recent past, about 2 per cent of the entire population of the Republic of Ireland left the country in a single

Piaras MacÉinrí and Paddy Walley, *Labour Migration into Ireland*, Dublin: Immigrant Council of Ireland, 2003. www.immigrantcouncil.ie. Copyright © 2003 Immigrant Council of Ireland. Reproduced by permission.

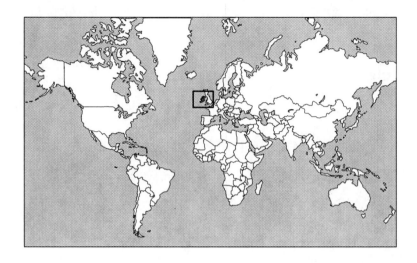

year (70,600 persons in the twelve-month period April 1988 to March 1989). This peak came at the end of a dismal decade during which nearly half a million people emigrated. The failure of successive governments to create a society able to provide for all of its citizens was matched by an equal failure to address the needs of those who were obliged to leave. Government funding for emigrant welfare organizations remained extremely meagre until the 1990s and a major Task Force Report on Emigration was not published until 2002. It remains to be seen whether its principal recommendations will be implemented.

The Celtic Tiger Economy

In contrast with earlier decades, the 1990s, the period of the so-called 'Celtic Tiger' economy, was characterised by significant economic growth, fuelled in large part by a policy of wage restraint achieved though a series of partnership-based agreements. This economic growth translated into job creation on a scale never previously experienced in Ireland.

Whereas just over 1.1 million people were at work in the Irish economy in 1988, this figure had increased by more than half a million by 2000. The growth in labour demand initially led to a significant fall in Irish unemployment rates as well as an increase in the number of women in paid employment. When employment growth is tracked against immigration it is evident that rapidly increasing employment in the early 1990s was not initially matched by increased immigration—in fact the rate of inward migration actually fell by more than 10,000 per annum between 1992 and 1994.

The figure for Ireland (population 3.9 million) of 47,000 [annual immigrants] would be the equivalent of well over 3 million annual immigrants to the US [proportionally].

The explanation is simple—those already available were the first to be drawn into the growing economy. However, by the late 1990s, the annual rate of job creation increased further and unemployment fell to about 4 per cent. From the middle of the decade onwards there is a clear correlation between increased employment growth and increased immigration.

Emigration rates have now fallen to an historical low of less than 20,000 per annum. Immigration, by contrast, has continued to rise, reaching peaks of more than 47,000 per annum in recent years and as will be explained later, this figure may in fact be an underestimate. To put this in some perspective, consider the United States (population 290 million) which consistently accepts a substantial annual intake of approximately 700,000 legal migrants from all parts of the globe. The figure for Ireland (population 3.9 million) of 47,000 would be the equivalent of well over 3 million annual immigrants to the US. The Irish rate of immigration is also high by EU [European Union] standards; only Luxembourg (which is an exceptional case, as a very small State where more than one third of the population is foreign-born) has a higher rate.

Who Are the New Migrants?

A substantial number of those included in the statistics are not immigrants in the strict sense, but returning Irish migrants.

The figure for returning Irish migrants peaked in 1999, at almost 55 per cent of all migrants; at present it is under 40 per cent. However, some of those migrants classified as foreign-born are the children of returning Irish migrants. While there is room for discussion about the statistics, it can be said with some confidence that the proportion of returning Irish migrants will continue to fall for one simple reason: The available 'pool' of would-be return migrants is itself shrinking, as Irish emigration has fallen in recent years. Those who left in the 1980s are now in their thirties or older. It seems reasonable to assume that most who might have wished to return and who had the possibility of obtaining employment in Ireland will already have done so. Future immigration is therefore likely to consist of a higher proportion of foreign-born individuals, the great majority of whom will have had no previous ties to Ireland. . . .

The figures for emigration and immigration between census years should be taken as a guide only and there is some evidence that the real level of immigration in recent years may have been higher than suggested. We know, for instance, that the CSO [Central Statistics Office] data for immigration suggests that the January to December 2001 figure for immigration from outside the EU and the United States was of the order of 15,000 to 15,500. Yet in the same year more than 29,000 new employment permits were issued (excluding US citizens) and 10,325 persons applied for asylum. This is before foreign students, who do not require employment permits, are taken into account, or the spouses and children (neither category of whom has an independent right to work) of those admitted with employment permits, work visas or work authorisations.

Therefore, the true figure for immigration from the 'rest of the world' (an outdated category anyway) must be considerably in excess of the CSO intercensal estimate and may have been closer to 40,000 than 15,000 in 2002. There is no reason to believe that the 2002 picture would have been substantially different, although there was a drop in new employment permits, from 29,326 to 23,326 (in real terms the drop was larger as about 3,000 of 'new' permits were actually for existing migrant workers who had changed employer). Asylum applications increased slightly, from 10,325 to 11,530 (provisional figure, January 2003). . . .

Despite some doubts about the reliability of the statistics, the trends are clear. The most salient point, for the purposes of this study, is the growing number of non-EU migrant workers. The aggregate annual number of employment permits, work visas and work authorisations is now more than 40,000. Figures to the end of August 2003 suggest there may be little change in overall numbers for [2003]. This may be compared with the far more modest figures, less than 12,000 including persons from Britain, for in-migration from other EU countries (although possible undercounting needs to be noted here as well).

The fact that migration from other EU countries into Ireland is less than migration from outside the Union is in line with EU experience generally. The *Social Situation in the European Union 2002* points out that of the 19 million non-nationals living in the 15 Member States, only about 30 per cent are nationals of another Member State. The same report, in a section headed 'population dynamics' points to other underlying demographic factors at work. Europeans are living longer and fertility is low. In fact, fertility rates in all parts of the EU, including Ireland, are currently below the population replacement rate; one of the lowest rates of all is in Italy. Put simply, better living standards in the regions and lower fertility mean that mass migration from any of the current EU

Member States is effectively over. The reality in most countries is very different, with a shrinking indigenous supply of people for the labour market. This explains why all EU countries are experiencing inward migration from third countries. Even though immigration cannot in itself solve the problems of low fertility and increasing age dependency in the EU, it is clear that managed immigration will play an increasingly important role in all EU Member States.

Economic Success Is Expected to Continue

It might be supposed that the general economic downturn which followed the events of 11 September 2001 (often referred to as 9/11) would lead to a revision of future immigration estimates. This type of forecasting is not an exact science. Even in the very recent past, the political instability caused by events in Iraq and the social and economic effects of the outbreaks of SARS [severe acute respiratory syndrome] in China, Vietnam, Singapore and Canada show that it would be oversanguine to assume that economic growth, and hence migration trends, can ever be predicted through a simple linear extrapolation of existing trends. The best that can be said is that there is no reason at present to suppose that immigration will not continue, although the level may fall somewhat.

The number of employment permits issued to new arrivals in the country fell in 2002 by more than 27 per cent (about 8,000).

The aggregate number of employment permits granted in 2002, at 40,321, was actually an increase on the figure for the previous year. However, this figure included 16,562 renewals; moreover, about 3,000 'new' permits were actually issued for existing migrant workers who had changed employer. Therefore, the number of employment permits issued to new arrivals in the country fell in 2002 by more than 27 per cent (about 8,000). However, this does not show that a drop in demand occurred, merely that a relatively high number of employment permit holders had their permits renewed, thus reducing the demand for new permits.

It is now more than likely that there will be a rise in unemployment in Ireland, at least for the short term. The market for tourism is particularly vulnerable, arising from the twin effects of the well-known reluctance of Americans to undertake foreign travel in times of uncertainty and the possible dangers of the spread of SARS. On the other hand, most commentators are in agreement that the medium- to long-term outlook for the Irish economy is relatively positive.

Finally, while there has been some suggestion that some employers were seeking to substitute Irish or other EU workers with cheaper non-EU labour, and while aspects of the employment permit system have been tightened up, we do not have evidence of wholesale labour substitution by non-EU immigrants. Many of the jobs being taken up in such areas as horticulture and meat processing are posts for which it is becoming increasingly difficult to find Irish or other EU workers. Evidence from other countries indicates that the 'substitution effect' of immigrant labour is not very significant. Having said that, there is little doubt that some unscrupulous employers and agencies have exploited migrant workers and in some cases denied them their rights, including the right to a minimum wage. Moreover, it should also be noted that if the effect of large-scale immigration to a particular sector of the labour market has been to drive down wages for that particular activity (usually a niche one) it is likely that workers in any such sector will continue to be marginalised and underpaid in relative terms and that the sector will therefore continue to be disproportionately one where migrant workers make up the labour force. This may be described as a form of substitution.

Countries with the Best Quality of Life

1 Ireland
2 Switzerland
3 Norway
4 Luxembourg
5 Sweden
6 Australia
7 Iceland
8 Italy
9 Denmark
10 Spain

TAKEN FROM: BBC, "Ireland Is Named 'Best Country'," November 17, 2004. http://newsvote.bbc.co.uk.

A More Diverse Population

The 1996 Census showed a population which was largely homogenous. If one excludes persons born in Britain (many of whom had Irish connections anyway) the total foreign community was small. Apart from the exceptional case of citizens of the United States (many of whom work in the multinational corporate sector), the numbers of non-EU citizens resident in Ireland at the time were very modest.

Since 1996, Ireland has received at least 147,000 foreign immigrants, of whom close to 57,000 (including almost 16,000 US citizens, with 41,000 in the 'rest of world' category) came from outside the EU. Although there may be room for debate about the numbers, there is the underlying reality of the volume of permits, visas and authorisations issued annually. If the higher figures discussed earlier turn out to be correct, especially for the period 2000 to 2002, the true figure for all non-Irish immigrants to Ireland since 1996 may be closer to 200,000, a remarkable 5 per cent of the population. This is without taking into account (a) family reunification and (b) undocumented migrants. There is also likely to be a degree of undercounting of students in this data.

The publication in June 2003 of some of the data from the 2002 Census provides further information on the number of foreign-born persons living in Ireland. Apart from the difficulties concerning possible intercensal undercounting already adverted to, the lack of a breakdown by ethnic background in the Census is a pity. Another difficulty, as pointed out earlier, concerns the numbers of foreign-born persons who are actually the children of at least one Irish parent and at least ethnically Irish. There was a question in the latest Census about nationality, as opposed to ethnicity, but this is a complex area and 1.3 per cent of those enumerated did not answer it. Of those who did, 91.6 per cent stated they were Irish and a further 1.3 per cent stated they had Irish and another nationality—it is probably not coincidental that the number reported as having been born in Northern Ireland [a country separate from the Republic of Ireland] is also 1.3 per cent. Of the 5.8 per cent who stated that they were not Irish or part-Irish in 2002, about half were British. The remainder came from all parts of the world.

A full 61 per cent of migrants ... were from central and Eastern Europe.

It is impossible, without more detailed cross-tabulations, to disaggregate the Census data in terms of the different categories of resident foreigners (migrant workers, asylum seekers, family reunification, students and so on). For the same reason, it is impossible to pronounce definitively on the intercensal immigration data and on the possibility that a degree of undercounting may have occurred. But one statistic which is worth citing is that mentioned earlier of the 41,000 from the 'rest of world' category (excluding the United States) in intercensal data for the period since 1996. The Census data for the slightly longer period 1996 to 2002 shows an increase in 'rest of world' from 24,552 to 97,159 (including non-EU Europe, Asia, Africa, the Antipodes and the Americas apart from US), a substantial increase of 72,607. Even allowing for the fact that many of these migrants may not be permanent, these figures are dramatic. . . .

A Diverse and Ubiquitous Community

[T]he characteristics of the new immigration are (a) diversity and (b) ubiquity. Migrant workers come from all parts of the world; the most strongly represented region is Central and Eastern Europe. They are employed in every sector of the economy, although clearly they are disproportionately present in certain sectors such as agriculture and horticulture; hotels and the catering industry; medical and paramedical care; and unskilled employment of various kinds. . . .

In short, Ireland has moved, from being one of the most homogenous countries in the EU, to a country with a rate of change which is almost unparalleled in speed and scale.

While migrant workers are found in all sectors of the economy, a large number of workers are concentrated in un-skilled or low-skill employment in services, catering, agriculture and fisheries, and industry. . . .

On the one hand, there is a remarkable spread of migrant workers. . . . On the other hand, a full 61 per cent of migrants . . . were from central and eastern Europe; a significant proportion of these are from the ten countries which will shortly become members of an enlarged EU from 2004. It is also clear that about 25 per cent of these migrant workers are from central and eastern European States which will *not* be part of the next EU enlargement process.

Questions must be asked about the nature of the recruitment process and whether unregulated intermediaries play an excessively influential role. It is difficult to understand why the largest single category of migrant workers is from Latvia, closely followed by Lithuania. How is it that the official statistics list only four Palestinian migrant workers, including one renewal, whereas anecdotal evidence from the Migrant Rights Centre in Beresford Place indicates that up to 100 Palestinian individuals and families live in the inner city area of Dublin? Questions need to be asked about the recruitment process, the adequacy of data being gathered and the potential level of undocumented migrant workers in Ireland. . . .

In sum, migration into Ireland on a substantial scale is very recent but its impact has been significant. Migrant workers, their families, refugees with full status and others with leave to remain are present in every sector of the Irish economy and in every part of Ireland. Irrespective of developments in the coming years, substantial numbers are here to stay.

It is sometimes argued that immigration somehow shows that emigration is a 'thing of the past'. In fact, as the CSO figures make clear, in examining age cohort depletion for the 15 to 24 age group, 'even in the most recent census period when average annual net inward migration exceeded 25,000, the 15 to 24 age group continued to record net losses due to emigration'. This must be a matter of concern. Ireland's economy may be increasingly knowledge-based, but there are many who continue to feel excluded.

Some Low-Income Countries Depend on Remittances from Migrant Workers

Dilip Ratha

In the following viewpoint, the author explores the impact of re-mittances on poor countries. In some instances, earnings sent back home by migrants are one of the main sources of revenue for individuals and families. The author also presents suggestions to lower the costs of transferring remittances from one country to another. Such reforms can be a way to increase the flow of money and further aid underdeveloped states. Ratha is employed by the World Bank as a senior economist.

As you read, consider the following questions:

1. According to the viewpoint, how many steps are usually involved in remittance transactions?
2. What percentage of GDP [gross domestic product] did remittances account for in Somalia in the late 1990s?
3. As identified by the viewpoint, what are some of the main problems created by regulations on the transfer of remittances?

When Migrants send home part of their earnings in the form of either cash or goods to support their families, these transfers are known as workers' or migrant remittances.

Dilip Ratha, "Remittances: A Lifeline for Development," *Finance & Development*, vol. 42, no. 4, December 2005, p. 42. Republished with permission of Finance & Development, conveyed through Copyright Clearance Center, Inc.

They have been growing rapidly in the past few years and now represent the largest source of foreign income for many developing countries.

It is hard to estimate the exact size of remittance flows because many transfers take place through unofficial channels. Worldwide, officially recorded international migrant remittances are projected to exceed $232 billion in 2005, with $167 billion flowing to developing countries. These flows are recorded in the balance of payments; exactly how to record them is being reviewed by an international technical group. Unrecorded flows through informal channels are believed to be at least 50 percent larger than recorded flows. Not only are remittances large but they are also more evenly distributed among developing countries than capital flows, including foreign direct investment, most of which goes to a few big emerging markets. In fact, remittances are especially important for low-income countries.

International remittance receipts helped lower poverty ... by nearly 11 percentage points in Uganda, 6 percentage points in Bangladesh, and 5 percentage points in Ghana.

The Process of Remittance Transfer

A typical remittance transaction takes place in three steps. In step 1, the migrant sender pays the remittance to the sending agent using cash, check, money order, credit card, debit card, or a debit instruction sent by e-mail, phone, or through the Internet. In step 2, the sending agency instructs its agent in the recipient's country to deliver the remittance. In step 3, the paying agent makes the payment to the beneficiary. For settlement between agents, in most cases, there is no real-time fund transfer; instead, the balance owed by the sending agent to the paying agent is settled periodically according to an agreed schedule, through a commercial bank. Informal remittances are sometimes settled through goods trade.

The costs of a remittance transaction include a fee charged by the sending agent, typically paid by the sender, and a currency-conversion fee for delivery of local currency to the beneficiary in another country. Some smaller money transfer operators (MTOs) require the beneficiary to pay a fee to collect remittances, presumably to account for unexpected exchange-rate movements. In addition, remittance agents (especially banks) may earn an indirect fee in the form of interest (or "float") by investing funds before delivering them to the beneficiary. The float can be significant in countries where overnight interest rates are high.

Remittances are typically transfers from a well-meaning individual or family member to another individual or household. They are targeted to meet specific needs of the recipients and thus, tend to reduce poverty. In fact, World Bank studies, based on household surveys conducted in the 1990s, suggest that international remittance receipts helped lower poverty (measured by the proportion of the population below the poverty line) by nearly 11 percentage points in Uganda, 6 percentage points in Bangladesh, and 5 percentage points in Ghana.

How are remittances used? In poorer households, they may finance the purchase of basic consumption goods, housing, and children's education and health care. In richer households, they may provide capital for small businesses and entrepreneurial activities. They also help pay for imports and external debt service, and in some countries, banks have been able to raise overseas financing using future remittances as collateral.

The Economic Implications of Remittances

Remittance flows tend to be more stable than capital flows, and they also tend to be counter-cyclical—increasing during economic downturns or after a natural disaster in the migrants' home countries, when private capital flows tend to decrease. In countries affected by political conflict, they often provide an economic lifeline to the poor. The World Bank estimates that in Haiti they represented about 17 percent of GDP [gross domestic product] in 2001, while in some areas of Somalia, they accounted for up to 40 percent of GDP in the late 1990s.

There are a number of potential costs associated with remittances. Countries receiving migrants' remittances incur costs if the emigrating workers are highly skilled, or if their departure creates labor shortages. Also, if remittances are large, the recipient country could face an appreciation of the real exchange rate that may make its economy less competitive internationally. Some argue that remittances can also create dependency, undercutting recipients' incentives to work, and thus slowing economic growth. But others argue that the negative relationship between remittances and growth observed in some empirical studies may simply reflect the counter-cyclical nature of remittances—that is, the influence of growth on remittances rather than vice-versa.

Remittances may also have human costs. Migrants sometimes make significant sacrifices—often including separation from family—and incur risks to find work in another country. And they may have to work extremely hard to save enough to send remittances.

The Burden of Transaction Costs

Transaction costs are not usually an issue for large remittances (made for the purpose of trade, investment, or aid), because, as a percentage of the principal amount, they tend to be small, and major international banks are eager to offer competitive services for large-value remittances. But in the case of smaller

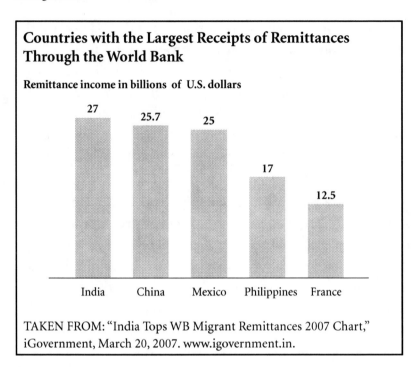

Countries with the Largest Receipts of Remittances Through the World Bank

Remittance income in billions of U.S. dollars

India	China	Mexico	Philippines	France
27	25.7	25	17	12.5

TAKEN FROM: "India Tops WB Migrant Remittances 2007 Chart," iGovernment, March 20, 2007. www.igovernment.in.

remittances—under $200, say, which is often typical for poor migrants—remittance fees can be as high as 10–15 percent of the principal.

Cutting transaction costs would significantly help recipient families. How could this be done? First, the remittance fee should be a low fixed amount, not a percent of the principal, since the cost of remittance services does not really depend on the amount of principal. Indeed, the real cost of a remittance transaction—including labor, technology, networks, and rent—is estimated to be significantly below the current level of fees.

Second, greater competition will bring prices down. Entry of new market players can be facilitated by harmonizing and lowering bond and capital requirements, and avoiding over-regulation (such as requiring full banking licenses for money transfer operators). The intense scrutiny of money service businesses for money laundering or terrorist financing since the 9/11 [2001] attacks has made it difficult for them to operate accounts with their correspondent banks, forcing many in the United States to close. While regulations are necessary for curbing money laundering and terrorist financing, they should not make it difficult for legitimate money service businesses to operate accounts with correspondent banks.

An example of where competition has spurred reductions in fees is on the U.S.-Mexico corridor where remittance fees have fallen by 56 percent.

An example where competition has spurred reductions in fees is on the U.S.-Mexico corridor, where remittance fees have fallen by 56 percent from over $26 (to send $300) in 1999 to about $11.50 now. In addition, some commercial banks have recently started providing remittance services for free, hoping that would attract customers for their deposit and loan products. And in some countries, new remittance tools—based on cell phones, smart cards, or the Internet—have emerged.

Third, establishing partnerships between remittance service providers and existing postal and other retail networks would help expand remittance services without requiring large fixed investments to develop payment networks. However, partnerships should be nonexclusive. Exclusive partnerships between post office networks and money transfer operators have often resulted in higher remittance fees.

Fourth, poor migrants need greater access to banking. Banks tend to provide cheaper remittance services than money transfer operators. Both sending and receiving countries can increase banking access for migrants by allowing origin country banks to operate overseas; by providing identification cards which are accepted by banks to open accounts; and by facilitating participation of microfinance institutions and credit unions in the remittance market.

Governments have often offered incentives to increase remittance flows and to channel them to productive uses. But such policies are more problematic than efforts to expand access to financial services or reduce transaction costs. Tax incentives may attract remittances, but they may also encourage tax evasion. Matching-fund programs to attract remittances from migrant associations may divert funds from other local funding priorities, while efforts to channel remittances to investment have met with little success. Fundamentally, remittances are private funds that should be treated like other sources of household income. Efforts to increase savings and improve the allocation of expenditures should be accomplished through improvements in the overall investment climate, rather than targeting remittances. Similarly, because remittances are private funds, they should not be viewed as a substitute for official development aid.

Chinese Immigrants in Hong Kong Are Socially Excluded in the Globalization Age

Law Kam-yee and Lee Kim-ming

In the following viewpoint, the authors examine how immigration policy has changed in Hong Kong. Hong Kong was traditionally open to migrants from mainland China, however, changes in the economy have made the region less welcoming. As a result, immigrants have a variety of economic and social problems. Law Kam-yee and Lee Kim-ming are both scholars at City University, Hong Kong.

As you read, consider the following questions:

1. How much was the fine to hire illegal immigrants in Hong Kong in the 1980s?

2. According to the authors' analysis, what was the major challenge of the "brain drain" crisis?

3. In what types of occupations are new arrivals in Hong Kong most likely to work, according to the authors?

In May 1999, the Hong Kong Special Administrative Region (SAR) government requested a reinterpretation of certain provisions of the Hong Kong Basic Law from China's National People's Congress in order to prevent a flood of immigration

Law Kam-yee and Lee Kim-ming, "Citizenship, Economy and Social Exclusion of Mainland Chinese Immigrants in Hong Kong," *Journal of Contemporary Asia*, vol. 36, no. 2, January 2006, pp. 217–226, 228. Reproduced by permission.

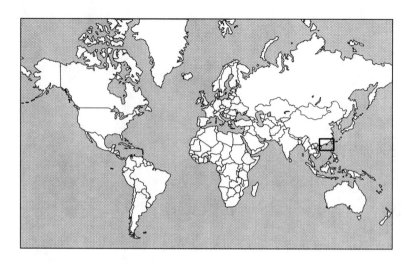

of Mainland children born to Hong Kong people. The reinterpretation of the Basic Law stirred up great contention within Hong Kong about the legal system and the autonomy of Hong Kong governance. But this controversy of the right of abode (ROA) is not purely an issue of "constitutional crisis." More seriously, it is an indication of social exclusion that has been constituting and reconstituting Hong Kong society since the late 1970s. . . .

Restrictions Lead to Illegal Immigration

China's Great Leap Forward and the collectivisation movement in agriculture during the late 1950s led to widespread starvation. Consequently, a large number of immigrants who did not have valid exit permits issued by the Chinese authorities, illegally fled to Hong Kong. This was the first wave of illegal immigration from China into Hong Kong since the imposition of immigration control by quota in 1950. From the 1960s onwards, until the 1980s, immigration was mainly illegal because Mainlanders had great difficulty obtaining exit permits, especially after the beginning of the Cultural Revolution. Even with the large inflow of illegal immigrants, David Podmore has contended that Hong Kong's population increase was mainly due to natural causes rather than immigration. According to the 1961 Census Report and the 1966 By-Census Report, the proportion of the population born within Hong Kong in 1921, 1931, 1961, and 1966 were 26.7%, 32.5%, 47.7%, and 53.8%, respectively. These figures show that by the 1960s, Hong Kong had become a more localised society, with more than half the population locally-born. . . .

Although the natural increase rate was quite high between 1950 and 1970, there was still a serious shortage of unskilled labour because of rapid labour-intensive industrialisation. Though the state indeed policed the Chinese border to reduce illegal immigration, the government exercised discretion in allowing these illegal immigrants to register and stay in Hong Kong whether they had been apprehended by the police or not. As [J.F.] Destexhe remarks, "Hong Kong's model for discretionary immigration control resembles that of countries which do not officially admit that they take worker migrants, but do so in practice." Nonetheless, the control was tightened from 1974 onwards. The Hong Kong state discontinued its actual practice of allowing all Chinese immigrants to stay in Hong Kong and replaced it with the "Touch-Base Policy" in 1974. According to new policy, those arrested illegal immigrants were repatriated to China and those who successfully evaded capture and subsequently established a home with relatives or found accommodation in urban areas (i.e. "touched base") were allowed to stay.

Although about 60% of Hong Kong's population is locally born, as an immigrant society, many Hong Kong residents have family ties in China.

The Open Door Policy

The "Touch-Base Policy" finally came to an end when China adopted the "Open-Door" policy in 1978. China's economic reform gradually eroded social and political controls at the local level, especially through the relaxation of the household registration (*hukou*) system, thus making population movement easier. Consequently, Hong Kong was again bombarded by an onslaught of illegal immigration that was even more massive than the one in the early 1960s. The state recognised that the existing immigration policy could no longer control the influx. Thus the Hong Kong state announced the abolition of the Touch-Base Policy on 23 October 1980; all illegal immigrants were subject to repatriation. Besides, the Immigration Ordinance was amended with urgency on the same date of the announcement. The amended Ordinance required all people residing in Hong Kong to carry identity cards or some other acceptable proof of identification at all times, otherwise, a maximum fine of HK$1,000 would be levied. Moreover, the new law also imposed heavy fines, the maximum of which was HK$50,000 or imprisonment for one year, on employers who hired illegal immigrants. Accompanying the amendment of the Ordinance, the Hong Kong government and the Chinese government reached an agreement to restrict the issuance of OWP [One-Way Permits] to 150 a day. This daily quota was subsequently revised downwards to 75 in 1983 and remained the same for ten years.

After the abolition of the Touch-Base Policy, the only way for Mainland Chinese to migrate to Hong Kong was to obtain the OWP. Even so, it remained common for illegal immigrants to cross the border. There are two forms of illegal immigrants. Besides OWP, the Chinese authorities can issue an unlimited number of Two-Way Permits (TWP), which allow holders to visit Hong Kong for the purpose of visiting family or doing business but require that they return to China after a designated period. However, the two-way permit system creates a loophole for illegal immigration. There are numerous overstayers. For instance, in 1991 there were 22,566 Mainlanders, 5% of which were TWP holders who overstayed. Many of the female overstayers aimed at giving birth in Hong Kong so that their children would be Hong Kong residents. Another mode of illegal immigration is the illegal entry by sneaking into the territory by land or by sea. Although the Hong Kong government has tightened border control since the 1980s, many illegal immigrants were successfully smuggled into Hong Kong by well-organised criminal networks to labour in construction sites, factories, and service establishments like eateries.

The problem of immigration through illegal entry ... has been greatly reduced in the 1990s. In the 1990s and 2000s, the most hotly debated issues concerning immigration are the labour importation policies and the ROA of spouses and children of Hong Kong residents who stay in the Mainland. Hong Kong's labour importation policies can be dated back to the late 1980s and early l990s when Hong Kong experienced acute labour shortages in many sectors. The General Labour Importation Scheme was introduced in 1989 on the basis of an industry quota system. In light of the rise in the unemployment rate the government terminated the General Scheme in October 1995 and replaced it with the Supplementary Labour Scheme. But in July 1990, the Special Labour Importation Scheme was introduced to facilitate the timely completion of the new airport. These labour importation policies, though welcomed by business, have been condemned by labour interest groups for creating unemployment among Hong Kong's workers as well as lowering the wages.

Although about 60% of Hong Kong's population is locally born, as an immigrant society, many Hong Kong residents have family ties in China. Indeed, most legal immigrants and overstayers come to Hong Kong for family reunion. The large number of overstayers is basically caused by the daily OWP quota system. The processing of applications for OWP has been poorly managed by the Chinese authorities: corruption has been widely reported; eligibility criteria are not applied consistently; and some eligible applicants have to wait for a very long time for approval. Most importantly, the Chinese authorities treat applicants individually rather than treating a family as a whole. As a result, there have been many young children being issued OWP, but not their mothers. This creates numerous single-parent families, and defeats the purpose of family reunion.

The median monthly family income for new arrivals is about 34%–46% of the overall Hong Kong median household income.

The End of Colonialism

Dreams of family reunion were greatly stimulated by the handover of Hong Kong's sovereignty to China in 1997. According to the Basic Law (Hong Kong's constitutional document) . . . children of permanent Hong Kong residents have the right of abode in the SAR. Just after the handover ceremony, a number of children of permanent Hong Kong residents who "illegally" stayed in Hong Kong went to the Immigration office to claim their ROA. As a result, on 9 July 1997, the Provisional Legislative Council quickly amended the Immigration Ordinance in a way that Mainlanders are required to hold OWPs, which are issued by the Chinese authorities, before they could exercise their ROA in Hong Kong. As for children born in the Mainland to the people of Hong Kong, one of their parents must be a Hong Kong permanent resident at the time of the birth. The amendment made a lot of ROA claimants who had "illegally" re-united with their families confront the fate of repatriation to the Mainland.

After numerous ROA court cases, on 29 January 1999, the Court of Final Appeal (CFA) gave a landmark judgement that these Mainland claimants were eligible for ROA. Nevertheless, the government immediately released an estimated and exaggerated figure of 1.67 million people in China who were eligible for entry, and threatened that if the CFA ruling were to be implemented, it would have great negative impact on Hong Kong's overall economy, employment, and various social services and facilities, like housing, education, medical, and health and welfare services. As a result, public support and sympathy for the claimants on their right of abode collapsed almost overnight.

Nonetheless, OWP is not the only way that Mainlanders can gain residence status in Hong Kong. For a privileged group of skilled workers, professionals, and overseas Chinese originally from the Mainland, they can migrate to Hong Kong by employment through various channels. One such method is to stay in Hong Kong continuously for seven years. Once they have done so, they are eligible to apply for permanent resident status. Various schemes have promoted this.

First, because of the "brain drain" in the late 1980s, in September 1990, the colonial government and the Chinese authorities reached an agreement that Chinese citizens who had resided overseas for two years or more could enter Hong Kong with employment visas. Presumably, those persons are high level talents with overseas exposure and are desirable to Hong Kong during the "brain drain" crisis. Second, Mainland enterprises established in Hong Kong are allowed to recruit employees from the Mainland without any quota limitation. Third, in March 1994, a Pilot Scheme for the entry of 1,000 Mainland professionals was introduced. Entry was restricted to graduates of the Mainland's 36 key tertiary institutions who also had relevant working experience. Later, an Admission of Talents Scheme was carried out after the new Hong Kong SAR government decided to promote Hong Kong's technological development. The scheme is quota-free and non-sector specific, and the successful candidates can also bring along their families to Hong Kong.

The Social Exclusion of the New Chinese Immigrants

Even though the ROA issue clearly indicates that the right of many new immigrants to family reunion, which is granted by Basic Law, has been denied, it constitutes only a small part of the social exclusion experienced by new immigrants. By the time of the handover in 1997, Hong Kong people had been deeply divided, despite the fact that these social divisions were temporarily submerged by the economic boom in the 1980s. And, with the impact of the Asian Economic Crisis, and the end of Hong Kong's economic bubble, divisions were exacerbated.

As Hong Kong's economy has become "post-industrial," just like other global cities, income distribution has become increasingly unequal. In 1986, the lowest decile group earned only 1.6% of total household income. The figure decreased to 1.1% in 1996. The highest group, however, earned 35.5% of total household income in 1986, a figure which increased to 41.8% in 1996.... The income gap continued to widen during late 1990s. In 1999, the 200,000 families in the lowest income bracket earned an average income of HK$3,000 per month, while the average family income was HK$70,000 per month for the top 200,000 families with the highest income. The high income bracket average is 23 times that for the low income bracket, as compared to having been only 13 times as much in 1996. The 2001 Population Census shows a wider gulf between rich and poor. The percentage of poor families—those earning less than HK$6,000 a month—rose from 10.8% in 1996 to 12.5% in 2001, while only 24.9% of households made more than HK$30,000 a month in 1996, rising to 29% in 2001. Meanwhile, families in the middle range of incomes fell from 64.4% in 1996 to 58.6% in 2001.

Income Disparity for New Immigrants

New immigrant families constitute a major proportion of Hong Kong's impoverished underclass. Newly arrived families earn much less than the average income of Hong Kong families.... The median monthly family income for new arrivals is about 34%–46% of the overall Hong Kong median household income for years from 1998 to 2003. Over half of

Hong Kong Seeks Talent and Skills

The Admission Scheme for Mainland Talents and Professionals was implemented on July 15, 2003. The objective of this scheme is to attract qualified Mainland talent and professionals to work in Hong Kong in order to meet local manpower needs and enhance Hong Kong's competitiveness in the globalised market. This scheme has no sectoral restrictions and allows intra-company transfer of senior managers and professionals. It also caters for the entry of talent and professionals in the arts, culture and sports sectors as well as those in the culinary profession so as to enhance Hong Kong's status as an Asian world city. As at the end of 2006, 14,155 talent and professionals were admitted under the scheme.

The Quality Migrant Admission Scheme has been implemented since June 28, 2006. The scheme is quota-based and operated on a points-based system. It seeks to attract highly skilled or talented persons from the Mainland and overseas to settle in Hong Kong in order to enhance Hong Kong's economic competitiveness in the global market. Successful applicants are not required to secure an offer of local employment before taking up residence in Hong Kong. They may also apply to bring in their spouse and unmarried dependent children below the age of 18 under prevailing dependant policy. As at end of 2006, a total of 83 applicants were allocated quotas.

"Hong Kong: The Facts, Immigration," November 2007 www.gov.hk.

the new immigrant families have an income that is less than half of the overall Hong Kong median family income.

Other than lower family income, the educational level of the new arrivals is also, on average, lower than that of the

Hong Kong population. . . . About 90% of the Mainland children aged 15 and over only attain secondary school educational level or below. Almost 30% of them have only primary school education or below. Comparing those entitled to ROA and those not entitled to ROA (after the re-interpretation of the Basic Law by China's National People's Congress in 1999), it is found that the latter have lower educational levels than the former. That means the latter group is even more vulnerable to economic disadvantages. This was one of the main reasons why the SAR government resisted granting ROA, claiming that ROA for poorly educated Mainlanders would increase Hong Kong's unemployment rate by 2%, and would threaten Hong Kong's high-tech and high value-added industrial development strategy. Henry Tang, then Executive Councillor and chairman of the Hong Kong General Chamber of Industry, estimated that unemployment would double if the government failed to stop the "flood" of poorly educated Mainland children born to Hong Kong people.

According to a survey . . . in 1997, 65% [of] employers admit that new arrivals were employed mainly due to their lower pay in comparison with locals.

The trend for new immigrants to be mainly of people with lower educational attainment still continued. In 1996, only 10.7% of new immigrants have tertiary education, while the figure for their local counterparts was 15.2%, about 40% higher than the new immigrants'. Five years later the proportion of new immigrants with tertiary education dropped to 5.7%, while the figure for locals was three times higher than that.

The new arrivals' disadvantages in the labour market are shown by the sectors in which they work and by their skill levels. From the 1996 data . . . new arrivals are mainly concentrated in either the sunset industries (such as manufacturing) or the low-paid and low-skilled service sector (wholesale, retail, import/export trades, restaurants and hotels). Their most frequent occupations are low-skilled ones; nearly half of the new arrivals are elementary workers, service workers, and shop sale workers. However, less than one quarter of the overall Hong Kong population works in these occupations. Moreover, almost 30% of the whole population are managers, administrators, professionals, and associate professionals, but only 15% of the new arrivals are in this category. . . .

[There is] an obvious income inequality between the new arrivals and the whole working population according to their highest educational attainment; as the educational attainment gets higher, inequality becomes more serious. Indeed . . . the disadvantaged labour market position of new arrivals is due to local people's discrimination against their educational attainments. According to a survey conducted by Human Resources Management Association in 1997, 65% [of] employers admit that new arrivals were employed mainly due to their lower pay in comparison with locals. This result is confirmed in another study; 40% of the new arrival respondents report lower wage and poorer welfare than their local counterparts. Even worse, 26% of the respondents have experienced rejection from employment simply due to their status as new immigrants.

The 2001 Population Census further demonstrates that the labour market situations of new arrivals are worsening. One reason for this is the decline of Hong Kong's manufacturing sector. The percentage of the labour force in manufacturing shrank from 47% in 1971 to 14% in 1996, and has continued to decline. Few capitalist economies have experienced such a rapid decline in the size of their industrial labour force. However, this decline has been even quicker and has had an even more drastic impact on new immigrants. In 1996, manufacturing was still the second largest employment sector for new immigrants (25.3%). By 2001, the percentage shrank to 10.4%.

Even if new arrivals can retain their jobs, these jobs are now concentrated in the low-skill, low-paid, and unstable service sector (e.g. retail, catering, and shop sales). There has been an increase in the proportion of the new arrivals working in those sectors, rising from 42.9% to 51.9% between 1996 and 2001. These rates have been greater than for the Hong Kong population as a whole. The declining situation for new immigrants can also be seen in the decline in the percentage of the new arrivals working as managers and professionals. The figure declined from 10.3% in 1996 to merely 3.9% in 2001; there has been no significant change for the overall Hong Kong population over the same period. On the other hand, the percentage of the new arrivals working in elementary occupations and working as service workers and shop sales workers rose rapidly from 47.3% in 1996 to 65.6% in 2001. It may be inferred that Hong Kong's economic restructuring towards a post-industrial economy and a global city has meant both structural downgrading and marginalization for new arrivals.

Japan's Economy Is Increasingly Reliant on Immigrants

Tony McNicol

In the following viewpoint, the author asserts that Japan's aging population is creating a growing demand for new workers and that immigrants are the best means to meet that need. McNicol examines the impact of the increasing number of immigrants from South America and how the Japanese government has begun to alter immigration policy to attract new groups. However, the author also notes that there are a number of hurdles for immigrants because of Japanese laws and customs. McNicol is a journalist and photographer who lives and works in Japan.

As you read, consider the following questions:

1. According to a United Nations report, by how much will Japan's population have declined in 2050?
2. Which does the author identify as the two largest immigrant groups in Japan?
3. What does McNicol report to be Japan's current birth rate?

Toyohashi is a medium-sized city in the middle of Japan. Local residents will tell you that their home city has a population of about 400,000, makes some of Japan's most de-

Tony McNicol, "Future Imperfect: Japan's Immigration Policies and the Winds of Change," *Japan, Inc.*, vol. 48, October 2003. Reproduced by permission of Japan Inc. www.japaninc.com.

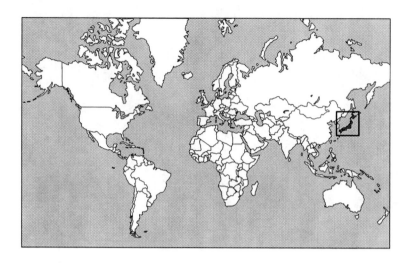

licious chikuwa (fish cake), and has an excellent surfing beach. They might even point out Toyohashi's futuristic Shinkansen station.

In short, Toyohashi is an average sort of place in a conservative and some might say ultra-Japanese part of Japan. But Toyohashi also has an energetic and conspicuously un-Japanese population: 10,000 South American immigrant workers, most of whom are Brazilians and Peruvians.

To fill the gap [in workers] completely through immigration, the nation would have to welcome an average of 381,000 per year all the way to 2050.

The Japanese Population Needs Immigration

What makes Toyohashi special is that it could possibly provide a template for the future of the nation as a whole. A UN [United Nations] report on replacement migration and declining birth rates estimates that if present trends continue, Japan's population will have declined by 22 million in 2050. To fill the gap [in workers] completely through immigration, the nation would have to welcome an average of 381,000 foreign workers per year all the way to 2050. Even with only a moderate influx of immigrants, every city in Japan could become another Toyohashi.

Is this economically and politically feasible? Those who think not are already casting about for alternatives. A demographic sea change which some argue is an economic necessity would mean that the immigrant population of Japan would swell from around 1 percent now to 17.7 percent by the middle of this century.

Of the nearly 2 million foreigners in Japan now, over half are Korean and Chinese, many of whom live in long established communities. Of the other million, over 300,000 are recently arrived Brazilians and Peruvians.

Sergio Okamoto arrived in Toyohashi in March 1990, close on the heels of new visa rules designed to encourage immigration by Brazilians, Peruvians and Argentines of Japanese ancestry. Born in Brazil to Japanese parents, Okamoto speaks fluent Japanese, Portuguese and English. At first, and like most South Americans, he found work in a factory. But now he works for a recruitment company supplying workers to a Toyohashi factory.

By some estimates, in 2050 Japan will have more than 33 million additional aged persons needing care.

Foreign Workers from South America

According to Okamoto, there is plenty of work for South Americans, recession or no recession. Foreign workers are still almost the only ones ready to do the most difficult, unpleasant and often dangerous jobs. Despite high unemployment in Japan and competition from some often over-qualified and desperate Japanese workers, it is still possible to find work paying [yen] 300,000 to [yen] 350,000 per month (including overtime).

Most of the Brazilians employed by Okamoto's company work 40 to 50 hours overtime per week, saving money to send home.

"If you stay here for a couple of years, you can buy a house, buy land and have capital to start a business [in Brazil]."

Professor Hiroshi Komai of Tsukuba University in Ibaraki has studied immigration into Japan. He says that Brazilians are no longer confined to the factories and have started finding other types of work—everything from being golf course caddies to caretakers for the aged.

In short, the immigrant economy is hollowing out just like the rest of the Japanese economy. Manufacturing jobs are going east to China, and South Americans are turning to the service sector. Japan's public policy planners in the early 90s may have imagined immigrants sweating unseen through automobile and electronics factory night-shifts, but a decade on many are working in shops, restaurants and offices—not least in the small economy of services catering to the immigrant communities themselves.

With its 15,000-strong immigrant community, Toyohashi may well become a model for the rest of Japan. But one major difference, says Komai, is critical: Future immigrants are unlikely to be South American. "The resource of the Japanese population in Latin America is already exhausted."

The newcomers are more likely to be from poorer countries elsewhere in Southeast Asia. Komai believes that the government may decide to open up the geriatric care sector to Asiatic foreign immigrants. By some estimates, in 2050 Japan will have more than 33 million additional aged persons needing care.

The Economy Needs Skilled Laborers

However, Komai doesn't believe that this sector alone can provide enough work for the immigrants Japan will need to sustain its population—and its tax income. What's more, the demand for general unskilled labor has been shrinking for the last ten years.

"The industrial structure has already changed," Komai says. "We have no capacity [to absorb unskilled immigrants]."

He says the die was cast when Japan shied away from large-scale immigration at the beginning of the 90s—and the nation's manufacturers found cheap labor in China.

So with as many as 17 million new residents to find by 2050, the Japanese government is now considering a different kind of immigration. For a number of years it has been chasing highly skilled foreign workers—mainly for the IT [information technology] industry.

Pasona-Tech is an IT recruitment company founded in 1998 and based in Tokyo. When the Japanese government reacted to a shortage of homegrown IT workers by relaxing visa rules for foreign IT specialists, Pasona-Tech started recruiting eagerly from India. But today, of the 200 IT specialists on their books, over 170 are Chinese. Again, the change can largely be explained by the manufacturing exodus to China. Many tech companies straddle the Sea of Japan with their headquarters and research departments in Tokyo and their factories firmly ensconced in China.

To come to Japan, job seekers need high-level university qualifications from their own country or ten years of experience in their field. Pasona-Tech's Chinese job seekers are all graduates from universities in their own country, but this is very much the exception among highly skilled Chinese employees in Japan. Most have graduated from Japanese universities, many with scholarships from the Japanese government. According to the Ministry of Education, about a third of all foreign students in Japanese universities are Chinese.

Significantly, Japan is not attracting significant numbers of highly skilled graduates from Chinese universities themselves—or from universities from anywhere else in the world, for that matter. Instead, Japan is largely drawing from a small pool of foreign students committed to Japan because of their time spent in Japanese universities.

Komai sees this as a sad sign of Japan's failure to attract international talent. Unfamiliar management techniques and pay scales based on seniority put off potential immigrants. Highly skilled workers with families worry whether the Japanese school system will be able to teach their children English. Will their children be able to compete in the international job market when they grow up?

If Japan can't absorb unskilled immigrants and can't attract highly skilled immigrants, what can be done to fill the gap in the working age population?

Already one in five Japanese are over the age of 65.

Methods to Maintain the Working Population

One suggestion is to encourage people to work longer. Already one in five Japanese are over the age of 65. Aside from the drastic drop in overall population, Japan faces a potentially crushing burden on its pension system. At the moment, every retiree is supported by approximately five working-age adults. By 2050, the ratio is expected to be barely one to two.

According to the UN population division, in order to redress the balance completely, Japan could raise the retirement age to 77 years. Even now, senior citizens have an average 15 to 20 mostly healthy years left after they retire. Many are already turning to part-time or full-time work to supplement their income. Anyone wondering what a Japan full of senior citizen workers will look like should just flag down a taxi in Tokyo. According to Tokyo's largest private taxi drivers union, more than half of their members are over 60, and 10 percent are in their 70s.

Obviously, the most direct way to address falling population would be to try to raise the birthrate. At present, Japan's fertility rate is about 1.5 children per woman in Japan. Most of the world's developed countries are facing a similar problem. Italy, for instance, has an even more acute problem, with a birthrate of 1.2 children per woman.

Komai points out that Japan also has the lowest rate of extramarital birth in the developed world. Women who want children, but who don't want to get married, have no choice but to stay childless. Countries like Canada and some of the Northern European states have tried to break the link between marriage and childbirth in an attempt to raise fertility rates. But in Japan, the mostly married men in suits in the Diet [Japan's legislature] seem unwilling to explore this option. At least, not yet.

Immigrants Face Discrimination

Whether Japan produces more babies, employs more senior citizens, does both or does neither, it seems likely that the number of foreigners in Japan will continue to increase. But even so, many people of non-Japanese origin living in Japan feel that the government is doing little to combat deeply ingrained and institutional discrimination against them.

Debito Aruhido (born in the United States as David Aldwinckle) became a naturalized Japanese citizen in 2000. When an onsen [hot springs] near his home in Hokkaido put up signs barring foreigners, he protested and launched an ongoing court struggle.

He quickly discovered that Japan has no law on its statute books explicitly outlawing racial discrimination. Yet Aruhido won the first stage of his case against the onsen. In his words, the decision explicitly stated that "the onsen overdid it. It went beyond the boundaries of what is called 'rational

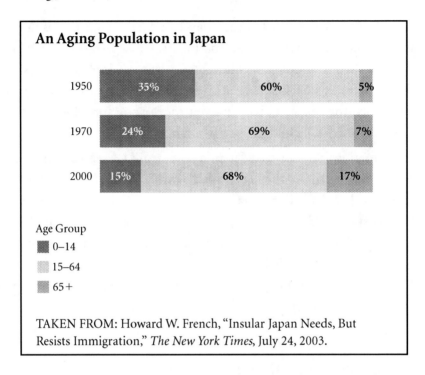

An Aging Population in Japan

1950	35%	60%	5%
1970	24%	69%	7%
2000	15%	68%	17%

Age Group
- 0–14
- 15–64
- 65+

TAKEN FROM: Howard W. French, "Insular Japan Needs, But Resists Immigration," *The New York Times*, July 24, 2003.

discrimination' in Japan . . . beyond the socially accepted bounds of discrimination. But it doesn't say that it is illegal because it is racial discrimination."

Aruhido believes that fundamental changes in attitude are needed. "There is this overwhelming canard that Japan is a mono-cultural, mono-ethnic society where there aren't any ethnic minorities. In the UN, Japan argues that the Ainu, the Burakumin and the Okinawans are not racially different, therefore the discrimination against them isn't racial."

He says that the government hasn't passed legislation against racial discrimination on the absurd grounds that no one would actually be protected by it. The vast majority of assimilated foreigners are Asian, and therefore can't possibly be victims of racial discrimination, in the government's eyes. If there is discrimination, it is because of the passports people carry—not their race.

The Future of Japan's Racial Identity

But with a swelling community of immigrant workers, how long can Japan maintain its self-image of a country united by racial identity? Will Japan take its first baby steps towards multiculturalism?

Apart from antiracism laws, Aruhido calls for immigrants to be able to keep their own passports when they become Japanese citizens. He also proposes a law to let children born in Japan automatically become Japanese citizens. "About half [of registered foreigners in Japan] are born in Japan. In any other developed country they would not be considered foreigners any more."

Daniel Alberto Harada, 26, works in a Toyohashi factory making roofs for Toyota cars. He works alongside twenty Japanese and seven Peruvians. He was born and grew up in Argentina, but came to Japan with his Japanese parents during an economic crisis in the mid 90s.

He has been in his job since 1997, on an assembly line with robots that slice through sheet metal with pressurized water. He says that although South Americans and Japanese in his factory have generally got along, the recent frictions make him sick. He works the night shift and accuses his Japanese coworkers of napping on the job.

"[The Japanese workers] think maybe because we are foreigners we have to only work, and that because they are Japanese, and we are in Japan, they get to sleep . . . Maybe they think we are robots."

The main problem for South Americans in the factories is their low status and poor conditions. The recruitment company system means that the factories are largely free from dealing with troublesome responsibilities, like providing severance pay or compensation in the event of injury.

"If I get fired, I get nothing," he says.

Challenges for Integration

Japan will have to move mountains to integrate large numbers of non-Japanese into the nation's economy and society. One part of Japan that seems to be trying hard is Nagano prefecture. Its reformist governor, Yasuo Tanaka, is well-known for opposing pork barrel construction projects in the prefecture, but now he's working to build bridges between the Brazilian and Japanese communities. In March, Tanaka received an award from the Brazilian state to thank him for his support of the 18,000 Brazilians in the prefecture.

One effort is the "Santa Project," an education project to support the children of immigrant children. Few Brazilians can afford to send their children to the few privately run Brazilian schools. Dropout rates are high among Brazilian children attending Japanese schools. A spokesman for the charity says that 17 percent of immigrant children in Nagano prefecture are not attending school. "Education is a basic human right," he says. "All children should be educated and [it] is crucial for the future of the children of immigrants. That's why we started the project."

This August [2003], Toyohashi held its annual summer festival. The city's main street was flooded with a colorful parade of floats, musicians and dancers. The festival has long included traditional Japanese dance and music, but recently a hint of South American carnival has crept into the proceedings. South American and Japanese dancers from the local samba schools showed off their moves together, adding an extra and by all accounts welcome flash of color.

Immigrant communities in Japan are still small. But those who wonder how Japan can ever become a multicultural nation are probably right to look for new policies and ideas. Perhaps in a few places, change has already arrived.

The United Kingdom's Immigration Improves the Economy

Shunil Roy-Chaudhuri

In the following viewpoint, the author extols the economic virtues of immigration for all countries and for the United Kingdom in particular. The viewpoint contends that immigrant workers generally help expand the economy by charging less for services or wages and thereby allowing people to spend money on other items. They also cause only minor losses to native workers. In addition, immigration actually helps keep taxes low because it reinforces negative sentiment toward the poor and working class, which, in turn, leads the public to be less supportive of social welfare programs. Roy-Chaudhuri is an economist and journalist.

As you read, consider the following questions:

1. What are the ways in which immigration can raise the wages of native workers, according to Roy-Chaudhuri?
2. With Russian migration to Israel, what was the effect on unemployment?
3. According to the viewpoint, what impact has racism had on income-tax rates in the United States?

Shunil Roy-Chaudhuri, "More Migrants Please!" *Investors Chronicle*, April 27, 2007. Copyright © 2007 FT Business. Reproduced by permission.

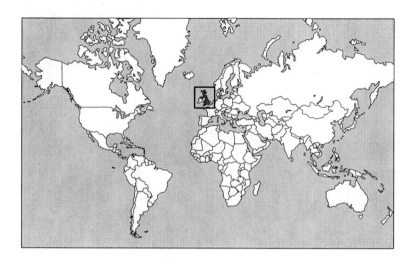

Immigration is at a record high. Official figures, which are probably an understatement, show that, in the last two years for which we have numbers, 1.15m[illion] people came to live in the UK—more than offsetting the 739,000 that have left.

But this is not the only record. Official figures also show that profit rates of non-oil companies at the end of 2006 hit their highest levels since current records began, and probably their highest since the early 1960s. Also, the misery index— the sum of the inflation and unemployment rates—will fall close to a forty-year low in [spring of 2007] . . . when [2006] rises in utility bills fall out of the inflation measure. And real interest rates—the gap between base rates and inflation—are near a twenty-six-year low.

Immigration and Jobs

All these records are connected. To see why, imagine there was no immigration, and you wanted to hire a plumber, but all plumbers were working flat out. What would happen?

The only way you could get a plumber would be to pay him enough to tempt him away from work he's already doing. This would cause inflation, as the prices charged by plumbers would rise. It would also mean that some valuable job would go undone, as the plumber moved from the lower-paying job to yours.

A country with immigration ... has higher output and lower prices than a country without immigration.

Now, consider what would happen if you could hire a Polish plumber. You wouldn't need to attract a British plumber away from his existing work, so plumbers' wages wouldn't rise. And there'd be more plumbing work done.

A country with immigration therefore has higher output and lower prices than a country without immigration.

What's more, because you don't have to pay more to get the job done, you've got more money to spend on other stuff. That creates work and profits for others. And because inflation doesn't rise, the Bank of England can keep interest rates down. That means low mortgage rates and hence higher consumer spending. Again, that creates work and profits.

Better still, low interest rates increase capital spending. That increases profits in the short run, and creates even more jobs in the long run.

This, however, is not the only reason that migrant workers are a good thing. Some complement existing workers, which means they can raise natives' wages directly. If an Albanian roofer joins a workforce, roofs are put on houses more quickly, so plasterers and electricians don't have to wait to start work. So they get more done and earn more. If a French anaesthetist joins us, surgeons can get more work done. And if an Italian IT [information technology] expert arrives, lawyers can get more work done because they spend less time cussing their computers. In such cases, supply and demand both grow. Again, profits are higher, without causing inflation.

There is, of course, a third situation: immigrants may directly compete with native workers. If so, the latter suffer either lower wages or job losses. But, even in this case, the losses are only temporary. Lower wages mean lower prices. That means consumers have more to spend on other things. If, say, cleaners' wages fall as a result of competition from immigrants, their clients have more money to spend on other things—say, DIY [do it yourself] equipment. As they spend this money, jobs are created in DIY stores. And, lower prices mean lower interest rates. That raises investment, and hence jobs, in the long run.

On average, a one-percentage-point rise in the proportion of immigrants in the labourforce cuts native jobs by 0.024 per cent.

Immigration's Influence on Native Jobs Is Small, if Not Positive

So, which of these outcomes is truest? Sure, there's anecdotal evidence for our third situation. But, although anecdotes are good journalism, they're a lousy basis for thinking about the world. A survey by Simonetta Longhi at the University of Essex has concluded that the effect of immigration upon native jobs was "negligibly small". On average, a one-percentage-point rise in the proportion of immigrants in the labourforce cuts native jobs by 0.024 per cent.

Indeed, even a flood of migrants doesn't displace native workers. Philippe Legrain, author of *Immigrants: Your Country Needs Them*, points to Israeli experience. After the collapse of communism, Russian Jews fled to Israel, swelling the working-age population by 15 per cent between 1990 and 1997. During this time, unemployment among native Israelis fell.

Instead, it seems to be our first two outcomes that are the true ones. Christian Dustmann of University College London has studied the impact of immigrant workers on native British ones and concluded that "there is little evidence of overall adverse effects of immigration". If anything, he says, effects on wages are "positive but statistically poorly determined".

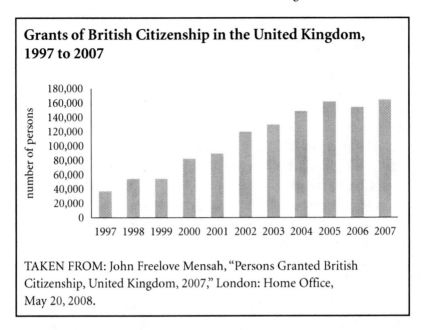

Grants of British Citizenship in the United Kingdom, 1997 to 2007

TAKEN FROM: John Freelove Mensah, "Persons Granted British Citizenship, United Kingdom, 2007," London: Home Office, May 20, 2008.

International evidence corroborates this. In a study of immigration into the US between 1990 and 2004, Giovanni Peri of the University of California at Davis concludes: "Average wages of natives benefit from immigration."

Indeed, not even MigrationWatch, the pressure group campaigning for "moderate and managed" immigration, claims that natives suffer economically from immigration. In a recent report, it said the impact of immigration on GDP [gross domestic product] per person was "minimal". Not negative, just minimal. And this ignores the long-term benefits of lower inflation and interest rates and higher capital formation.

So, immigration is a good thing. It increases output, profits, and employment, and helps keep down inflation and interest rates. Monetary policy committee member David Blanchflower says: "Most people would probably agree that extra immigrant workers in the economy would raise supply potential."

Even immigration minister Liam Byrne has spotted this. "Our long boom without inflation would have been impossible without migration," he said recently.

Some Doubt Immigration's Positive Influence

All that's happening here is yet another manifestation of [father of modern economics] Adam Smith's famous invisible hand. The free decisions of rational people help make everyone better off. Let's put this another way. Many of our clothes are now made in the Far East where wages are low. Most of us regard this as a wholly good thing. Only a cretin or a European Commissioner—the two are hard to distinguish—would propose banning such imports. But such a ban is, economically speaking, the same as a ban on immigration. In both cases, we stop labour entering the country. It's just that, in one case, the labour is embodied in a T-shirt, and in the other it's embodied in a person.

Here's Philippe Legrain again: "The economic benefits of immigration are analogous to those of international trade. In effect, immigration allows rich countries to import low-cost, low-skill labour-intensive services from poor countries. By doing so, we reduce the costs of such services, which allows more people to benefit from them."

Restricting immigration is just like restricting imports—a way of making us poorer.

All of this raises the question: why, if it's so clear that immigration is good for jobs, do so many people think otherwise?

There are numerous cognitive biases at work. One is a simple fallacy: the lump of labour error. This is the idea that there's only a fixed among of work to do, so that if foreigners (or machines) do it, there'll be fewer jobs for the rest of us. But this, as centuries of growth in wealth and population proves, is just plain wrong in the long run.

There's also the status quo bias: we prefer things as they are and distrust change and unfamiliarity. And there's an adverse halo effect: because immigration creates problems in some areas—overcrowding on public transport, the breakdown of older communities—we assume it must be a problem in all respects. But it isn't necessarily so.

Immigrants who are well-integrated into native society do more damage to natives' wages than those who remain separate.

There are, however, a couple of more legitimate reasons for skepticism about the economic benefits of immigration. First, some types of worker do see wages fall as a result of competition from immigrants. Professor Peri estimates that wages of unskilled Americans have fallen as a result of immigration. And Dr. Dustmann estimates that UK-born workers with middling qualifications have suffered a fall in employment.

Both agree, however, that the gains to other, higher-skilled, native workers are greater than these losses.

Secondly, Pia Orrenius of the Federal Reserve Bank of Dallas has found that the longer immigrants stay in the US [United States], the greater the downward effect they have on the wages of unskilled natives. This is because long-stay immigrants become more like native Americans, and so become closer substitutes. This suggests a delightful trade-off: immigrants who are well-integrated into native society do more damage to natives' wages than those who remain separate. That's not something you hear from those who call upon immigrants to become better integrated into British society.

The Economy Benefits Further from Discrimination

Why should investors care about the minority of workers who do lose?

Backlash. That's why. Political pressure to compensate these losers might lead to higher taxes or to tougher restrictions on immigration, either of which would hurt profits.

Here, though, lies what is—from the point of view of people like us—another great benefit of immigration. It actually reduces demand for income distribution.

There's lots of academic research to support this. Yale University's John Roemer has estimated that American voters' racism has reduced income-tax rates by around 15 percentage points. Chicago University's Enzo Luttmer says "Welfare benefit levels are relatively low in racially heterogenous states." Just compare Scandinavia or Japan or South Korea to the US or Brazil.

The mechanism here is simple. If people think income and redistribution will benefit a different ethnic group, they'll oppose it. As Harvard University's Alberto Alesina says: "Racial animosity in the US makes redistribution to the poor, who are disproportionately black, unappealing to many voters."

This is depressing for anyone with a rosy view of human nature. But it's good news for investors: it helps keep taxes down.

There are a couple of other ways in which investors should, in principle, benefit from free immigration.

First, it should increase the incentives for native-born workers to become more skilled. No one, after all, wants to be so poor that they have to live in the worst areas, or so badly trained that their job can be better done by an immigrant. Immigration, then, acts as a boot up the backside.

Also, it must be remembered that the case for free immigration is primarily one of liberty. Employers should be free to hire whom they want, landlords to have the tenants they want, and workers to take the jobs they want.

If a government doesn't respect these basic liberties, isn't it also likely to violate investors' freedoms too? Wouldn't you, as an investor, feel safer under a government that promoted economic freedom rather than restricted it? Economic research suggests you should. Marshall Stocker of US fund management company Sanderson and Stocker estimates that countries enjoying rising economic liberty also see better stock-market performance. "Cross-country equity returns are directly related to increases in economic freedom," he says. And freedom to move jobs is a basic economic freedom.

So, it's clear that free immigration is a good thing for the economy and stock market.

This doesn't, of course, mean immigration is wholly good. Perhaps immigration reduces social cohesion. Australians give us earache about the failings of our cricket team and Portuguese win our football trophies. These are all heavy burdens. But let's be clear—the economic effects of immigration are almost wholly beneficial.

Periodical Bibliography

The following articles have been selected to supplement the diverse views presented in this chapter.

Janusz Bojarski — "Problems of Black Labor, Illegal Immigration, and Money Laundering in Poland," *Journal of Money Laundering Control*, August 14, 2007.

Felix Büchel and Joachim R. Frick — "Immigrants Economic Performance Across Europe—Does Immigration Policy Matter?" *Population Research and Policy Review*, April 2005.

Business and Finance Magazine — "Spain Must Deal with Tragedy of Immigration," August 26, 2004.

Jack Citrin and John Sides — "Immigration and the Imagined Community in Europe and the United States," *Political Studies*, March 2008.

The Economist — "A Turning Tide," June 28, 2008.

Richard Florida — "America's Looming Creativity Crisis," *Harvard Business Review*, October 2004.

Sally Goodman — "Getting Mobile in Europe," *Nature*, March 2007.

Carol Matlack — "How Spain Thrives on Immigration," May 10, 2007. www.businessweek.com.

Peter Merrick — "Backlogs Cause Canada to Lose Thousands of Business Immigrants," *The Lawyers Weekly*, November 14, 2004.

John Rossant — "The EU: Choking Off Its New Blood," *Business Week*, March 15, 2004.

Matthew Stern and Gábor Szalontai — "Immigration Policy in South Africa: Does It Make Economic Sense," *Development Southern Africa*, March 2006.

Peter Wehner — "Keeping Them Out, Letting Them In," *Commentary*, July 2008.

**GLOBAL**VIEWPOINTS

CHAPTER 3

Immigration and National Identity

European Union Members Need to Actively Promote Assimilation of Immigrants

Amitai Etzioni

In the following viewpoint, the author argues that both countries and immigrants need to do a better job of assimilating new arrivals into the broader fabric of society. Different types of immigrants, including asylum seekers, are examined in terms of their motivations and impact on society. Also, a proposal to better integrate immigrants through revisions to the school system is presented. Amitai Etzioni is a scholar who writes on community and societal issues, and he is the author of more than fifty books.

As you read, consider the following questions:

1. What grants international asylum seekers the right to protection in another country?

2. What is the difference between humanitarian immigration and utilitarian immigration, as described by Amitai Etzioni?

3. According to the viewpoint, what are some examples of how diversity has enriched societies?

The starting point for a new way of thinking about immigration is the recognition that *no one* has a *right* to be in another person's country any more than one has a right to

Amitai Etzioni, "The Rights and Responsibilities of Immigrants," *Quadrant*, vol. 50, no. 6, June 2006, pp. 9–13. Copyright © 2006 Quadrant Magazine Company, Inc. Reproduced by permission.

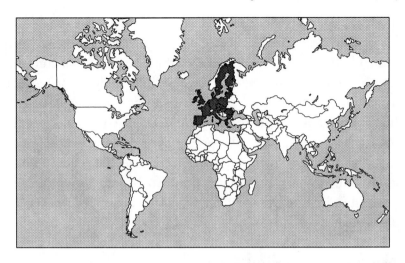

move into their home. The Universal Declaration of Human Rights recognises no such claim, nor does established international law, the draft constitution of the EU [European Union], or any other authoritative body of law or ethics. Entry into a country is a *privilege* one can earn—and should be able to earn, under reasonable terms set by the community one aspires to join—but not a right all foreigners can justly claim.

Immigration Is a Privilege

People flourish when they are members of communities. To nurture these communities, the bonds of affinity must be sustained, a limited but significant set of shared values (or moral culture) must be fostered, and a sense of shared history and shared future must be cultivated. This is true not merely for small, local communities but also for nations, commonly understood as communities invested into states.

One day we may have regional communities like the EU or even a global community. However, currently and for the foreseeable future, nations often are the most relevant communities when dealing with immigration. To ignore this fact is to confuse wishes for a better world with the sociological reality in which we must function even as we seek to change

111

it. Hence, anyone who seeks to join a particular nation to improve their personal life must be willing to buy into the communal bonds and moral culture of the given national community, assume the burdens of its past and the obligations tending to its future. We shall see that this requirement does not entail that immigrants be blended down, disappear into the prevailing society, assimilate to the point they are no longer distinct, or be prohibited from working to change their new homelands. However, they must labour to become members in good standing or their quest to become a member can be justly denied.

Asylum Is a Limited Right

Genuine asylum seekers are an exception. They do have a right to shelter. This right, however, is more limited than is often recognised. Asylum seekers are entitled—by international law and elementary justice—to a safe haven, to protection when their life is endangered or when they are truly escaping the threat of torture or other serious physical injury. However, this right does not entail a right to a particular shelter, in a particular nation. When a woman knocks on one's door seeking shelter from an abusive husband, one ought to take her either into one's own home or to a shelter for abused women. That is, the right to protection does not include the right to a specific, let alone five-star, shelter. Genuine asylum seekers need to be protected—some place. (I am speaking on moral grounds. Some argue that international treaties require that a nation allow asylum seekers who knock on its doors to stay in that particular country. If this is the case, these treaties ought to be renegotiated.) Hence it is legitimate to transport asylum seekers to safe havens in developing nations as long as they are safe in these nations and these nations serve as willing hosts.

A side benefit of such a policy is that it would greatly curtail the motivation to fake a claim of asylum and prevent those whose claims have not yet been vetted from taking root in a community in which many of them will eventually be denied residence. Moreover, such a policy would greatly enhance the process of granting asylum to those who genuinely need it, for the sharp decline in fake applicants would vastly accelerate the processing. It would also lead to a much less hostile and suspicious view of applications than now, when most are applying under false pretences, undermining the reputation of those truly in urgent need.

We take it for granted that a child will learn the national language (or languages).

One may argue that fake asylum seekers are merely poor people desperate to improve their lives, and that under such conditions many of us would resort to concocting lies and forging documents. Hence, one should not deport them. To deal with this and related issues it is useful to distinguish between what might be called *humanitarian immigration*, the primary purpose of which is to help the individuals involved, and *utilitarian immigration*, whose main purpose is to help the economy of the nation involved. While humanitarian immigration seeks to help people most in need—often from deprived and vulnerable backgrounds—utilitarian immigration seeks out young healthy workers, people with large amounts of capital, and those with skills in short supply. Of course some immigrants qualify on both accounts, but many do not, and above all the examination of the issues involved is muddled when we do not draw the suggested distinction.

If we allow numerous fake asylum seekers to stay in a given country in the name of compassion, we end up allowing people in who are not the most in need: In effect, they jump the queue in front of many who seek entrance and who are more in need. A nation should make the scope of humanitarian immigration proportionate to its compassion, but at the end of the day there will always be many more people who seek admission than can be admitted, and hence criteria for selection—immigration filters—need to be established and heeded.

Humanitarian v. Utilitarian Immigration

It should be further noted that as far as humanitarian immigration is concerned, often many more people would be helped if a given nation would join others to pressure rogue countries (Sudan for instance) to treat all their citizens humanely. Along the same lines, progress would be made if the "have" nations increased the investments, credits and grants that they extend to people in need in their countries of origin rather than transplanting those people en masse to new countries. The promise of this course of action is higher the greater the cultural and educational differences between the country of origin and the new homeland.

To put it more bluntly: It is not compassionate to take someone with little preparation for modern workplaces, city life, not to mention democratic politics, out of some hinterland—and plant them in one of our cities on the naive assumption that they are going to acculturate and live happily ever after. Indeed *both* sides suffer, as we have witnessed recently in French cities and ought to admit is taking place in many other cities. In short, the more compassionate a nation is, the more resources it should dedicate to helping those most in need, often in their home country, and the more it should ensure that those who do immigrate are truly among those most in need.

Utilitarian immigration is different. Because these immigrants are to be chosen on the basis of qualifications that include their ability to find and hold jobs (say they have skills in short supply), youth, high level of preparation (for example, they have passed language tests)—they are much more likely to be successfully integrated into their new homeland economy and society. Bringing in immigrants on humanitarian grounds and assuming they will act like utilitarian ones generally does not work.

Immigrant Education Is Crucial

When a child is born to a family whose lineage harks back hundreds of years in the same national community, whose parents, grandparents and great-grandparents have all lived and served in the same community, whether a local or a national one, the community still lays a considerable set of demands on that child. We take it for granted that the child will learn the national language (or languages). Also we require that the child attend school in which familiarity with and commitment to society's moral culture, history and future will be taught and fostered.

Above all, from an early age the child will learn to behave in line with the basic prevailing norms of respect for rules and the law, authority figures, non-violence and mutual tolerance. Although this is not always fully recognised, a good part of teaching in pre-school, kindergarten and primary school is dedicated to character and behavioural development (what social scientists call "socialisation", making children into prosocial beings) rather than just the three R's [reading, writing, and arithmetic]. Think about a child who is a bully or shows racial or gender bias and you will see my point. The staff will work long and hard with this child to introduce him to the societal norms and encourage him to internalize them.

From my days as a parent, I still remember the constant reminder, "Use your words", for any child who showed the slightest inclination to use force against others, or "Use your indoor voice" for those who spoke in a louder or more agitated voice than the society considers appropriate. Numerous hours are spent in teaching children ways to work out differences by discussions rather than fights, to seek common ground, and to be empathetic.

There is no reason for a national community to expect less of immigrants than it demands of children born in that country. And, just as we use tests in schools, *citizenship tests* should be used to determine whether a person has mastered the national language, moral culture, and above all basic respect for law and mutual tolerance. Those who fail these tests may be given another test, say five years later, but they ought to be denied citizenship and residence if they fail repeatedly. Citizenship and residence should also be denied to immigrants who have been convicted of a crime, especially a violent one, have indulged in hate speech, or have abused their spouses or children.

There is little that will better serve to ensure that naturalized immigrants will be full members of the community than extensive citizen education followed by meaningful citizenship tests. Just as the appeal of being a candidate for joining the EU has driven many nations to work hard to democratise and respect human rights, the prospect of becoming a citizen will motivate many immigrants to learn the ways of their prospective new homelands.

Citizenship for immigrants cannot be based on blood lineage as it was in Germany, because then no preparation will suffice and hence a major source of motivation for pro-social conduct will be lost.

A Naturalised Citizen's Responsibilities

One may say that immigrants are people from disadvantaged backgrounds and that it is unfair to impose various requirements on them. However, one does no favour to immigrants when one does not encourage them to learn the language of the society they seek to join, to respect its laws, to forgo violence, and to buy into the basic values that all the members of the society are expected to share. If immigrants will not acculturate to this limited extent—I discuss shortly the many areas in which they are welcome to maintain their sub-cultural distinctions, in which particularism is welcome—they will suffer economically, socially and politically and so will the host society.

Certain conditions must be met in order for citizenship tests to have the desired effect.

Citizenship for immigrants cannot be based on blood lineage as it was in Germany, because then no preparation will suffice and hence a major source of motivation for pro-social conduct will be lost.

Spain, for instance, gives priority to immigrants from Spanish-speaking countries.

For the same reason, test requirements cannot be so high that only very few will have a realistic prospect of meeting them. One may use school levels as a guide; for instance one can expect a fourth-grade command of language, a fifth-grade level of history and so on. (American and the new British citizenship test requirements are set much too low and they test knowledge but not behavioural predispositions. In contrast, several Swiss cantons' informal criteria are much too high. Some fully acculturated, third-generation immigrants are still denied citizenship.)

Most importantly, tests are called for to ensure an inclination to respect the law and be tolerant of members of their new homeland who adhere to different beliefs. An immigrant's criminal record should weigh heavily in such considerations, but it should not be the only consideration. Designing a test of compatibility promises to be a difficult, but not impossible task. Employers and career counsellors often use analogous selection testing—they use a questionnaire to provide a psychometric assessment of a candidate's work-related characteristics and then compare those characteristics to the personality traits of an optimal employee.

The Advantages of Integration

Promoting integration of migrants into the host country would go a long way in alleviating the trade-off between economic and political considerations. In Europe, unemployment rates are typically larger for migrants, fostering natives' suspicion that migrants tend to ride on the welfare state. Similarly, migrants tend to earn less than natives, even after controlling for their individual traits, fuelling concerns that they depress wage levels. Under both counts, therefore, a better integration of migrants into the host country's labour markets would help dispel the concern about their impact and improve natives' attitudes.

Domenico De Palo, Riccardo Faini, and Alessandra Venturini,
"The Social Assimilation of Immigrants,"
Discussion Paper 2439, *The Institute for the Study of Labor,*
November 2006. http://ftp.iza.org.

One might argue that meaningful citizenship tests will screen out too many people when nations are in need of immigrants. However, *the need for immigrants does not dictate that those immigrants must come from backgrounds that make socialisation especially difficult.* Spain, for instance, gives priority to immigrants from Spanish-speaking countries. In any event, immigrants best prepare and face preliminary tests before they enter a given country—and pass meaningful citizenship tests before they become permanent members of the community of their new homeland, citizens of their new state.

Diversity Can Still Be Celebrated

If immigrants buy into the basic values, laws, and institutions of their new homeland, they should be allowed, indeed welcome, to diverge on other matters. There is no reason to insist that one and all enjoy the same cuisine, dance the same dances, express identical interests in terms of their countries of origin, or even pray to the same god. On the contrary, such diversity within unity enriches the society and helps better prepare it for a globalising world.

Some expect immigrants to assimilate to the point that they become indistinct from native citizens (this is a common expectation in France, for instance). Such a degree of assimilation is often difficult to achieve and unnecessary for social peace and good community and obviates the enriching effects of diversity. On the other end of the spectrum, there are those who call for multiculturalism according to which immigrants are free to maintain their cultures and resist socialisation into the prevailing national culture (which in effect most nations do have, although this culture never encompasses everyone).

Some multiculturalists even call for abolishing any sense of national identity, as Lord Parekh's Commission on the Future of Multi-Ethnic Britain has suggested. Accordingly, the United Kingdom would become a territory which English, Scottish, Welsh, West Indian, Pakistani and so on would inhabit like tribes or communities resting next to each other with little more in common.

The images used for depicting these two positions are telling. The first is that of a melting pot, in which all differences are melted down; the other is that of a salad in which various pieces are tossed together but each maintains its original colour and flavour.

As I see it, to reiterate because this is the essence of the position here advanced, if immigrants buy into what might be called the societal basics, they are not only free, but welcome to diverge on other issues. What belongs in the shared framework and what belongs in the realm of diversity is open to deliberation and change over time. However, it is clear that immigrants must accept the basic values of the society (for example, tolerance for people of different backgrounds, habits and religions, as well as respect for democratic policies and human rights), must obey the law, learn the nation's language(s), and share not only in the treasures history has bequeathed to the nation, but also in its burdens.

Just as when one joins a family, through marriage or adoption, one cannot say, "I am entitled to part of the assets but not the liabilities," so too when one becomes a member of a new society, one has to take the burdens of history along with the promises of the future. For example, as an immigrant to America I cannot claim that I had nothing to do with slavery and hence have no need to concern myself with making up for past injustices, and yet also claim that I am entitled to the rights that the Founding Fathers institutionalised. Similarly, a new German cannot pride himself on the achievements of Kant, Goethe and Bach but not also share responsibility for the Holocaust.

Subcultures Enhance the Whole

At the same time, every group in society is free to maintain its distinct subculture—those policies, habits, and institutions that do not conflict with the shared core—as well as a strong measure of loyalty to its country of origin, as long as this does not trump loyalty to the society in which it lives if these loyalties come into conflict. Cuisine, by itself of limited import, serves as an effective symbol for my point. Once upon a time, there was a national cuisine, although there were always local variations and changes over time. We still recognise national cuisines today, but the effects of immigration, globalisation, increased travel, and other factors have meant that in most cities a large variety of other cuisines are prepared and consumed both privately and in public places such as restaurants, conferences, and banquets. Nobody in his right mind would suggest that anything was lost in the process and that all the Brits (old and new) should be required to drink warm beer and eat shepherd's pie and boiled vegetables.

In short, the diversity of cuisine has enriched our lives rather than threatened our unity. The same holds true for many other items including not merely music, dance and clothing styles, but also our second or third languages, special knowledge and interest in one's country of origin, among others. The more new citizens bring special knowledge of and contact with parts of the world that native citizens have been less familiar with, the better one and all are.

The image of a mosaic captures the diversity within unity that I champion. A mosaic is enriched by a variety of elements of different shapes and colours, but it is held together by a single framework. This is not to say that the framework of the mosaic remains static; it can be recast and indeed it has been recast frequently throughout history. However, those who seek membership in a given community must buy into the framework, and those who are native members best respect those differences the framework justifies and indeed welcomes.

Diversity Within Unity (DWU) does not advocate that identities of the host country should be overriding, that they should wipe out the identities of immigrants or all of their loyalty to their countries of origin. But DWU does call for layered identities and loyalties, in which the more encompassing community (the nation or the European Union) would provide the overarching identities and loyalties within which various groups could maintain their sub-identities—for example, as Turkish-Germans.

The test comes when loyalties conflict. Will Americans from Panama fight for the United States if the United States invades Panama, or will they demand a right to sit out such a conflict? Will Turkish Germans take their cues on matters concerning national policies from Istanbul or Berlin? Dual citizenship is acceptable if it means that a person has rights in two countries and involvement in both—as long as there is no conflict between the two. But as a rule, a nation will demand that in such situations loyalty to it will take precedence.

All children from all backgrounds should be expected to attend the same classes for 85 per cent of school time.

A Restructuring of School Curricula

Education is of key importance for the future relationship between immigrants—and their children—and their new homeland. Different methods of schooling serve both as a powerful way to show how the DWU approach differs from other approaches and to show the implications of DWU for education in general. Unfortunately the ideal form of implementation that is discussed first here cannot always be followed, and hence a second-best approach is also outlined below.

The assimilationist model assumes that immigrants and minority members of society will be taught in public schools, that they will be taught basically the same material as other members of the society and more or less the same material as was previously provided. An unbounded diversity model calls for setting up separate schools—publicly supported—and distinct curricula for various ethnic groups from kindergarten to Year 12, such as, for instance, separate Muslim or Jewish schools, not merely as "Sunday" schools but as full-time schools.

A DWU approach, based on the concept of neighbourhood schools, suggests that ideally:

- All children from all backgrounds attend the same public schools and learn about each other as they interact not only in regular classes, but also in sports and other social activities.

- All children from all backgrounds should be expected to attend the same classes for 85 per cent of school time (this part of the processes fosters unity). The commonalities of sharing 85 per cent or so of the curriculum are intended to ensure that all members of the next generation are exposed to a considerable measure of the same teaching materials, narratives and normative content.

- Minorities should have major input concerning 15 per cent or so of the curriculum; this could be in the form of electives or alternative classes in which students particularly interested in one subject or history or tradition could gain enriched education in that area.

- Although teachers of all backgrounds should be welcome, requirements that children must be taught by teachers who are members of their ethnic group is not compatible with the DWU model. Teachers must be selected by educational authorities, meet professional standards, and cannot agitate for extremist religious or ideological viewpoints or any values incompatible with those that are part of the basic framework.

- The universal, unity-related content of the curriculum should be recast to some extent to include, for instance, more learning about minority cultures and histories.

- Bilingual education might be used, but only during a transition phase before mainstreaming begins and not as a continuous mode of teaching that is, in effect, segregated along ethnic lines. (Reference here is to education that is conducted in the languages of immigrants and not to educational policies in a country that has historically embraced two or more languages.)

- Teaching values is of particular concern. This issue is highlighted by the fact that many of the most contentious issues in schools, ranging from displacing crucifixes to requiring Muslim girls to wear swimsuits to banning Sikhs' traditional turbans, relate to religion. As previously discussed, schools must help develop character and teach basic values rather than merely being institutions for learning "academics". Classes that all pupils will be required to attend (the unity sector of 85 per cent plus) will include classes in basic civic values, such as respect for the constitution or basic laws, human rights, the merits of democracy, and the value of mutual respect among different subcultures. (These are to include civic practicums, such as doing community service, or play-acting as parliament or civil court.) Beyond that there ought to be room in the elective sections of the curriculum for teaching religion and secular humanism. Above all, character education benefits from community service, sports conducted with special attention to learning to play by the rules, and monitoring by older students of playgrounds, corridors and other shared spaces.

In some nations, private education is divided on religious lines—there are Catholic, Protestant and Jewish schools. These divisions are so deeply and so long ensconced that it is hard to imagine that a shift towards the ideal DWU education system is possible in the foreseeable future. In the meantime, it is important to ensure that 85 per cent of the curriculum of all private schools is the same, that all private schools transmit the basic shared values of the society to their students, and that no extremists will be allowed to agitate against the basic values of the society in private schools. To ensure adequate oversight it is best private schools are considered "deputised" by the state, rather than true private bodies. The state need not wait for them to violate a rule before it is entitled to act; it can be proactive in all the matters already listed. Also the DWU platform encourages private school students to interact with each other in social activities and community service.

There are numerous other issues to be worked out in the context of the DWU approach and much is to be learned from applying it. However I hope that the preceding discussion serves to both outline and illustrate the basic idea of the approach.

DWU acknowledges the feeling of the overwhelming majority of the citizens in Europe and many other nations from Japan to Peru; the feeling that immigration poses a challenge to national unity and the prevailing moral culture. But DWU also captures the attitude that immigrants can also be allowed, and are indeed welcome, to retain distinct characteristics as long as they buy into the basics.

Zimbabwe's Denied White Farmers Are Increasingly Welcomed in Neighboring Countries

Neil Ford

In the following viewpoint, the author analyzes the impact of white African migrant farmers. Most of these farmers left Zimbabwe after the government began a program by which it bought or seized large farms and redistributed the territory. In addition, a growing number of farmers have also left South Africa because of violence. Many neighboring countries have offered the immigrants opportunities to start new farms in efforts to improve agricultural production.

Neil Ford is a special correspondent for African Business.

As you read, consider the following questions:

1. Who owns the Mozambican land these migrant farmers now call home?

2. How should Angola anticipate new migrant farmers will impact unemployment, according to Neil Ford's speculation?

Neil Ford, "Africa Welcomes Zim Whites: White Farmers, Kicked Out of Their Agricultural Holdings in Zimbabwe, Are Finding a Warm Welcome in Other African Countries Even as Far Away as Nigeria. What Do African Governments Hope to Gain from Them?" *African Business*, December 2003, pp. 26–27. Copyright © IC Publications 2003. Reproduced by permission.

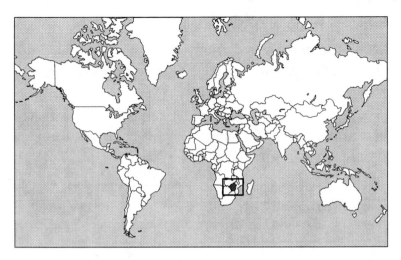

3. According to the viewpoint, in Malawi, what groups currently own 50 percent of the farmland?

Although the Zimbabwean government has clearly stated its desire to move most of the country's white farmers out of the agricultural sector, the farmers have found their services to be much in demand in the rest of the continent. While some have left Africa for the UK [United Kingdom], US [United States] or Australia and others have moved on to South Africa, some are being lured to other parts of the continent by African governments hoping that they can help generate export revenues and create employment.

The process of transferring Zimbabwean land away from the white farmers has occurred at the same time as southern Africa has suffered its worst drought for many years. The two events appear to have culminated in the popularity of the farmers elsewhere on the continent, as southern African governments appear convinced that the Zimbabweans can help rebuild their agricultural sectors.

Mutually Beneficial Opportunities

Angola, Mozambique and Zambia have all offered land to the farmers, although the packages on offer vary in their attractiveness.

In addition, Angola and Mozambique are both emerging from decades of warfare and are keen to return abandoned agricultural land to productive use.

Zimbabwe had only about 4,500 white owned farms prior to the land redistribution program.

Although Mozambique has enjoyed a far longer period of peace than its lusophone [Portuguese-speaking] counterpart, the agricultural sector has yet to recover. Accurate figures are difficult to come by but the Mozambican government claims that over one hundred white Zimbabwean farmers arrived during the course of 2002 alone, mainly taking up land near the Zimbabwean border. The white farmers do not actually own the land they work but act as concessionaires on state owned property. Although most of the immigrants have made a reasonable start, some have complained that the depth of local bureaucracy is hampering their efforts to establish viable enterprises.

Only 12% of state owned arable land is currently cultivated, with a massive 32m hectares of arable land lying idle, so there is plenty of acreage to give to the new arrivals. Soares Nhaca, the governor of the central Mozambican province of Manica, where most of the white Zimbabweans are farming, says that demand for land has reached such a level that he has asked other provinces to offer land to the white farmers. The province of Zambezia has already begun to offer acreage and others may follow, although it is unlikely that the flow of arrivals will increase as Zimbabwe had only 4,500 white owned farms prior to the land redistribution programme.

Conditions in Zimbabwe Are Driving out Health Care Professionals

The vast majority of Zimbabwean health professionals (68.0%) are considering leaving the country in the near future. In the case of nurses, the figure is as high as 71%.

The most likely destination (MLD) is the United Kingdom (29.0%). However, a sizable number prefer destinations within Africa (mostly South Africa followed by Botswana). Other fairly popular intended destinations include Australia, the United States, New Zealand and Canada.

Abel Chikanda, "Medical Leave:
The Exodus of Health Professionals from Zimbabwe,"
Southern African Migration Project, No. 34,
Queen's University (2005).

Angola has only emerged from conflict over the past couple of years and a great deal of the country's agricultural land remains virtually undeveloped, either because local farmers feared that any crops would be taken by one side or the other in the war, or because of the prevalence of land mines.

Angolans themselves would benefit from access to this land once it has been made safe, and land reallocation is certain to play a key role in persuading former UNITA [National Union for the Total Independence of Angola] fighters that they have a stake in the new Angola.

Many are currently frustrated, bored and living in the poverty of the resettlement camps and if they can rebuild their lives around a smallholding or farm then there is far less chance of a renewed outbreak of fighting. However, the Luanda administration appears convinced that white farmers could make a contribution to reestablishing farms and boosting exports.

It must also be admitted that the white owned farms provided a lot of employment to local people in Zimbabwe and the Angolan government may be banking on such job creation to absorb some of the country's landless millions. Reports in the Angolan press indicate that around 24,000 acres of land in the province of Huambo has been allocated to the new arrivals. The province was an important maize [corn] growing area until the outbreak of war.

The Challenges of Land Redistribution

While views vary on the rights and wrongs of the land redistribution programme in Zimbabwe, it cannot be denied that Zimbabwe gained a reputation as the breadbasket of southern Africa during the years of white control of the agricultural sector. Zimbabwean products were found across the southern half of the continent, from South Africa to Tanzania. The host countries trying to attract the white farmers seem to be relying on their ability to get the same results again.

At least one million people are estimated to have left Zimbabwe since the land struggle began.

Many of the white Zimbabweans left the country with little or no money and so have been forced to take out large loans in order to invest in their new farms. Although they usually receive the land for free, they need to purchase agricultural machinery, seeds and fertilisers, and must pay their new workers for months before the first harvest. Many plan to grow tobacco and so have been able to secure backing from international tobacco companies but others are able to invest little because they cannot raise loans as they do not actually own their land.

Elsewhere in the region, attitudes to the white farmers have been mixed. Around 120 farmers have moved north to Zambia, where many state-owned farms suffer from under-investment and have often been virtually abandoned. Malawi is also considering offering land to Zimbabwe's former white farmers. White farmers and British tea growing companies already own about 50% of the country's arable land.

A spokesperson for the Botswana government said last year that there was not enough land to give to the Zimbabweans but some richer farmers are believed to be considering setting up joint ventures with local farmers.

The scale of the migration of Zimbabwean white farmers should not be exaggerated, given that it comprises only a tiny fraction of all population movements in the region. At least one million people are estimated to have left Zimbabwe since the land struggle began, including many Mozambicans who had fled to Zimbabwe during the 1970s and 1980s because of fighting in their own country but who have now returned to a newly peaceful Mozambique.

In addition to trying to attract Zimbabwean farmers, countries like Mozambique are also encouraging their South African counterparts to take up acreage. Many South African white farmers have been attacked in recent years and some have already moved to other parts of the continent, encouraged by the fact that—unlike Zimbabwean farmers—they can sell their land, machinery, and livestock as a going concern before moving on, in a slow trickle of migration that has been compared to the Great Trek [a movement of Europeans from the Cape Colony] of the 1830s.

South Africa's Violence and Inequality

The report of a two-year study by the Human Rights Commission in South Africa into life on the country's farms was published at the end of August [2003]. The report paints a picture of a culture of violence on all sides and concurs with the view that the number of murders of white farmers is rising. It produced the startling statistic that 1,500 white farmers have been killed since the end of apartheid—at a rate of over

100 a year. However, such a figure should be put into the context of the overall very high murder rate in the country. The Commission report argues that criminal gain is the main motive behind such attacks, although revenge attacks and anti-white feeling also play a role.

The Commission also concluded that living conditions on the country's farms, which are still mainly owned and run by white South Africans, are very poor for the largely black workforce. Extreme poverty and limited access to health services and education are compounded by the limited application of the labour laws and incidences of violent attacks upon black workers are relatively common.

The use of child labour remains a particular problem. The report argues that assaults "are of such a nature and frequency as to indicate that there is a culture of violence in which acts are perpetrated in an environment of impunity." The report blames the culture of violence, alcoholism and the high murder rate on the huge imbalance in living standards between black and white South Africans, which is even worse in rural areas than in the towns.

While efforts to provide decent housing, piped water, electricity and improved health care to the South African masses have focused upon urban areas and the townships, living conditions on the country's many remote farms have barely improved. Moreover, government policies aimed at correcting the unfairness of the past have focused upon areas with higher population densities.

Migration Is Expected to Continue

The process of land reform has barely begun in South Africa but it is certain that some form of land redistribution will occur. A few examples of white farmers voluntarily entering joint ventures with their former farm labourers, handing over land or setting up profit sharing schemes do exist, but no large-scale change is expected until the government intervenes.

A group of white South African farmers toured Kwara state in the west of Nigeria in September [2003], following an invitation from the state government to both Zimbabwean and South African white farmers to relocate to the state. Not only did the state government fund the trip but it has also offered to give land for free to farmers who agree to move to the area on a permanent basis.

Kwara is one of the poorest states in Nigeria but it does have a great deal of fertile land. Although it is not known whether the land on offer is currently occupied, the state government obviously believes that the southern African farmers can create jobs and boost agricultural production. Although the idea of farmers relocating to Nigeria may seem fanciful, a handful has already moved to East Africa, including Uganda, so the idea cannot be ruled out.

The campaign to attract white farmers has caused some uproar in the host countries, particularly because of the number of landless families in rural areas across the continent. In any event, it will be interesting to chart the progress of the farmers in the years to come, as their success could encourage others to invest.

Canadian Pluralism Demands Compromise from Both Immigrants and Natives

Graeme Hamilton

In the following viewpoint, the author describes how some local communities in Canada are increasing efforts to integrate immigrants into the mainstream of the country's culture and traditions, but he contends that the national identity is not so easily defined. The small Canadian town of Hérouxville has adopted a "code of life" that they might present to potential immigrants, but Hamilton asserts that there is also much to be gained from the diversity that immigration brings. Hamilton is a journalist for the Canadian newspaper, the National Post.

As you read, consider the following questions:

1. What are some actions that are forbidden under Hérouxville's code of life?

2. From what area of the world do most immigrants to Quebec, Canada, originate?

3. What requirements do potential immigrants to the Netherlands face?

Graeme Hamilton, "The Hérouxville Code," *The National Post*, December 30, 2007. www.nationalpost.com. Copyright © 2007 CanWest Interactive Inc. and CanWest Publishing Inc. All rights reserved. Reproduced by permission of the National Post company, a Canwest Partnership.

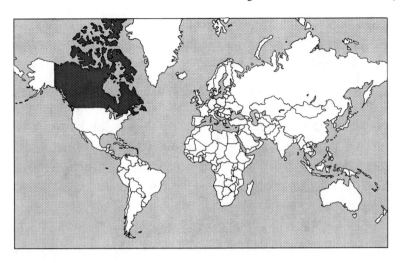

Sometimes, big ideas are hatched in little places. Over two decades, the village of Hérouxville in Quebec's Mauricie region was mentioned all of ten times in Montreal's *Gazette*. There were a couple car wrecks, a raid on deer poachers and some minor horse-racing successes from a local stable. Then last January [2007], the municipal council adopted a "code of life" telling would-be immigrants what's what, and suddenly Hérouxville (pop. 1,300) was shaping public debate in the province.

> *Since jihadists brought down the World Trade Center [in New York City] in 2001, there has been heightened suspicion of all Muslims and questioning of their commitment to the values of liberal democracies.*

The town was referred to in more than one hundred and fifty *Gazette* articles in 2007, and the story of the Hérouxville code made it as far as Fox News and the BBC [British Broadcasting Corporation]. The code's authors were criticized for offering a caricature of Islam, feeling obliged to declare that stoning women, burning them alive in public or dousing them with acid would not be tolerated. But to the dismay of intel-

135

lectuals in Montreal, Hérouxville's code struck a chord with many Quebecers. The town's stand was saluted by former premier Bernard Landry, and Mario Dumont, leader of the Action Démocratique du Québec, called it "a heartfelt cry."

Phrased awkwardly, in places offensively, the code gave expression to a fear felt elsewhere in Canada, and throughout much of the Western world: Have our societies gone too far in accommodating alien religious and cultural practices, to the point where our own values—and perhaps our security—are undermined?

It is not hard to see where the fear comes from. As declining birth rates in the West have obliged nations to open their doors more widely to immigrants, some clashing of new and old cultures was inevitable. Since jihadists brought down the World Trade Center [in New York City] in 2001, there has been heightened suspicion of all Muslims and questioning of their commitment to the values of liberal democracies. Terror attacks in Bali [an Indonesian island], Madrid [Spain] and London followed; cartoonists required police protection after they dared draw Mohammed. In an age of 24-hour news channels and instant Internet communication, all these events— plus the knowledge that countries in Muslim North Africa have become the greatest source of immigrants to Quebec— informed the Hérouxville view that Western values are under siege.

Immigrant Knowledge of National Identity

They were not alone in wanting to send a clearer message to people considering settling in their backyard. In 2006, then British Prime Minister Tony Blair gave a speech outlining immigrants' "duty to integrate," targeting "a new and virulent form of ideology associated with a minority of our Muslim community." The Netherlands, once considered the most open and tolerant nation in Europe, imposed a language test requiring prospective immigrants to show proficiency in Dutch before landing in the country (European Union countries, the U.S., Canada, Australia and Japan were exempted). A new video about life in Holland, used to screen potential immigrants, is not all windmills and tulips. There are shots of homosexuals kissing in public and a bare-breasted woman bathing, to gauge whether newcomers realize what they're signing on for.

Like the people of Hérouxville, most Canadians would like to know that immigrants coming here are prepared to live by our rules and embrace our identity. Where things get tricky is when we try to spell out the rules and sketch the identity. If Canada tried to produce a video capturing its essence, it would likely confuse immigrants so much they would be tempted to choose another destination.

"If people whose forebears arrived two centuries ago still haven't figured out a solid definition of what it means to be Canadian, how can Canada ask people arriving next week to pledge themselves to the cause?" pollster Michael Adams writes in his new book, *Unlikely Utopia*.

Thanks to a selective immigration policy that puts a premium on education, Canada does not have the social problems brought on by ghettos of unemployed immigrants in Europe.

Daniel Weinstock, a professor of political philosophy at Université de Montréal, said Canadians have no reason to be ashamed of the "thinness" of their identity. In fact, in today's world of increasing migration, it makes the country much better suited to absorb new arrivals.

"The recentness of our history doesn't saddle us with these identities that are sort of written into the very soil," he said. Thanks to a selective immigration policy that puts a premium on education, Canada does not have the social problems brought on by ghettoes of unemployed immigrants in Europe.

Immigration to Canada	
Year	**Number of Immigrants**
1997	214,293
1998	173,050
1999	189,741
2000	227,411
2001	250,600
2002	229,018
2003	221,339
2004	235,823
2005	262,231
2006	251,639

TAKEN FROM: Statistics compiled by editor.

Canadian Pluralism Prevails

Still, couldn't Canada use a "code of life" so there is no misunderstanding?

"We have it. It's called the Charter of Rights and Freedoms," Mr. Weinstock replied. "There ain't that many people in Montreal stoning people or throwing widows on the funeral pyre. All the things that are described [in the Hérouxville code] are illegal. . . . The more we try to define an identity that goes beyond the Charter, the more we find ourselves hitting against the deep pluralism that constitutes our society." Forget about how Quebecers would react to a made-in-Ottawa code; how would Calgarians feel?

Ronald Beiner, a professor of political science at University of Toronto, thinks most people grasp the ground rules without having them carved in stone. "The Canadian model involves a kind of reciprocity. On the side of the host culture there is a tacit undertaking not to freak out about people's cultural practices—if you see a woman wearing a hijab [head covering], for example. On the other side, the immigrant cultures don't freak out about the idea that their children are being exposed to a liberal society," he said.

"If both sides stick to that contract, there are benefits on both sides. The host culture gains the benefits of cultural diversity, which are huge. On the other side are the real benefits of freedoms for individuals that you get living in a liberal society."

Some things are clearly inadmissible, for example female circumcision and polygamy [marriage to more than one person at a time]. When a father is suspected of killing his daughter for her refusal to adhere to strict Muslim values, or when a group of youths are suspected of plotting terrorist attacks, the criminal justice system responds.

"There are certain ground rules, but within those there is space for people to continue, for at least a generation or two, to be faithful to the cultures they're coming from," Mr. Beiner said. "But there will not be some wall erected so you can carry on living in Canada as though you had never left Bangladesh."

And, to the disappointment of Hérouxville, neither can a wall be erected around their town, their province, or their country so they can continue living as though immigrants had never arrived.

Some Hungarians Seek to Expand Citizenship Outside Hungary's Borders

Mária Kovács

In the following viewpoint, the author explores a proposal to expand citizenship to immigrants and other ethnic Hungarians living outside of Hungary. The initiative would have allowed these Hungarians the full rights of citizenship, and it would have increased the number of citizens by an estimated one-third. However, the proposal faced opposition from both domestic groups and Hungary's neighbors and it failed in a 2004 referendum. Kovács is a professor at the Central European University in Budapest, Hungary.

As you read, consider the following questions:

1. According to the viewpoint, what was so innovative about the proposed 2004 referendum on dual citizenship?

2. What groups was the Hungarian dual-citizenship proposal designed to include?

3. How would dual citizenship affect the status of Hungarians living in non-European Union countries?

Mária Kovács, "The Politics of Dual Citizenship in Hungary," *Citizenship Studies*, vol. 10, no. 4, September 2006, pp. 431–434, 436. Copyright © 2006 Taylor & Francis. Reproduced by permission.

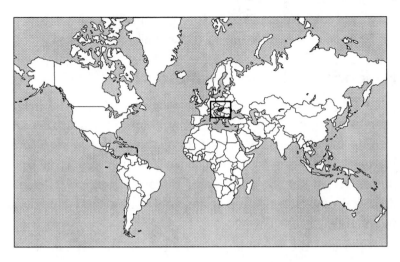

In Hungary the issue of dual citizenship has recently emerged as a controversial issue and, for a few months in 2004, it has even captured the center stage in politics. On 5 December 2004, six months after Hungary's accession to the European Union [EU], voters were asked in a referendum to decide whether Hungary should offer extraterritorial, non-resident citizenship to ethnic Hungarians living outside Hungary by lifting all residency requirements from among the preconditions of obtaining a second, Hungarian citizenship. The novel aspect of the proposal was not the introduction of dual citizenship itself, since the option of obtaining a Hungarian second citizenship had long been available for permanent residents within the country. The innovation would have been to remove all residency requirements from among the preconditions of obtaining a Hungarian second citizenship. The question posed at the referendum was as follows:

> Do you wish that Parliament pass a law which would enable an applicant who declares himself/herself to be of Hungarian nationality, but is not a Hungarian citizen and does not live in Hungary, to enjoy the right of preferential naturalization at his/her request, provided he/she can provide proof of his/her Hungarian nationality with the possession of a "Hun-

garian identity card" issued on grounds of Law LXII.19, 2001, or in any other way to be determined by the law.

Hungarians Abroad Are Many

Accordingly, Hungarians living outside Hungary's borders were to be granted the possibility of obtaining Hungarian citizenship merely upon declaring themselves to be of Hungarian linguistic affiliation at a Hungarian consular office, or upon possessing an identity card issued by the Hungarian state since 2002 for non-citizen Hungarians confirming their Hungarian nationality.

Although the referendum question left the precise criteria of eligibility open for future lawmaking, an approximation of potentially eligible claimants can be made on the basis of the size of transborder Hungarian ethnic minorities whose numbers are estimated at around three million. If Hungarians from all over the world were included, the number of potentially eligible claimants would rise to five million. Thus the number of those eligible for Hungarian citizenship would be augmented by at least a third of Hungary's current citizenry of ten million. Assuming, for argument's sake, that the majority of those made eligible by the reform would actually claim citizenship, the proportions of the resulting change would exceed the growth of Germany's citizenry after unification, but of course, without the corresponding territorial enlargement. Or to give another analogy, the resulting change would be proportionate to the entire population of Mexico being made eligible for United States citizenship.

This in itself points to the first specificity of the Hungarian story, namely that the dimension of Hungary's kin-minority problem is unusually large: nearly a quarter of all Hungarians live outside Hungary's borders in neighboring states. Other European nations with comparably large kin populations living abroad are Ireland, Italy, Finland, Austria, Belgium and Portugal, but Hungary is a special case insofar as minority Hungarians in neighboring states are, to a large extent, located in compact settlements on the other side of Hungary's borders.

The Referendum's Failure

The proposed reform failed to win a popular mandate in the referendum of 2004. But the movement towards citizenship reform is by no means exhausted. Powerful endorsers of the reform within the Hungarian political establishment, among them the chairman of the main right-wing party (FIDESZ), Viktor Orbán, have pledged to pursue the reform and to create non-resident dual citizenship in case of the electoral victory of the right in the 2006 elections. According to Zsolt Németh, chairman of the foreign policy cabinet of FIDESZ, Hungary should introduce non-resident dual citizenship despite the failed referendum, but only after a reform of Hungarian citizenship law that would establish two kinds of Hungarian citizenship, one that belongs to those who reside in Hungary and one that is extended to those who do not reside in the country. The president of the republic, László Sólyom also expressed sympathy for the initiative.

Meanwhile, the Federation of World Hungarians, the organization that had initiated the 2004 referendum, announced plans for a new referendum to be held in 2006. Meanwhile, in June 2005, the socialist-liberal coalition amended Hungarian citizenship law, introduced a new form of "national visa" for transborder Hungarians and shortened the process of naturalization for minority Hungarians moving into Hungary.

Debates over the Hungarian citizenship reform raised several contentious issues present in citizenship debates worldwide, but also brought forth problems that are specific to the East-Central European region. The Hungarian initiative was directed at external co-ethnic minorities living in neighboring states and at the Hungarian diaspora [people settled far from their ancestral homelands] living elsewhere in world. As such, the reform would amount to what Christian Joppke identified as the "re-ethnicization" of citizenship, a process in which states provide preferential access to citizenship to people, including non-residents, who are considered ethnic or linguistic relatives. Within Europe, such policies are pursued by countries including Germany, Portugal, Spain, Italy, and Greece. In the East-Central European region, Croatia and Romania introduced similar legislation. But while such reforms in Western and East-Central Europe may look similar in terms of the legal techniques involved, they are intended to address different concerns and thus carry different political and social implications.

In Western Europe, citizenship reforms aimed at the preferential treatment of ethnic relatives abroad mostly emerged in the context of migration and was adopted without drawing much international attention. As Christian Joppke put it, such reforms constituted a "little-noticed side plot" alongside more important reforms aiming at easing up access to citizenship, by receiving states, for ethno-culturally foreign immigrants. Even in a country like Spain where citizenship reforms have produced an elaborate regime for the preferential treatment of ethnic relatives abroad, these reforms were counterbalanced by measures easing up access to citizenship for ethnically foreign labor migrants.

In 1991 Romania created non-resident second citizenship for ethnic Romanians.

Issues Unlike Those Raised in Western Europe

As compared to Western immigration countries, the context in which the issue of preferential treatment of ethnic relatives has been raised in East-Central Europe is fundamentally different. Here, the defining events of the first decades following the collapse of Communist regimes had less to do with labor migration and all the more to do with the dissolution of multinational federations and the formation of twelve new states in the region. Therefore, unlike in Western Europe, in East-Central Europe, questions of membership, of who does and does not belong to the nation touch upon sensitive issues of state sovereignty and evoke problems of historically disputed borders and transborder ethnic-kin minorities.

For example, when, in 1991 Romania created non-resident second citizenship for ethnic Romanians in neighboring Moldova, the reform had been based on the expectation that Moldova, a successor state of the Soviet Union, would, in time, cease to exist as a sovereign entity and the country, that had used to be a part of Romania before its incorporation to the Soviet Union, would again be unified with Romania. At the same time, the ethnic Russian population of the separatist Transdnistrian region of Moldova was allowed by Russia to retain Soviet passports. Eventually, in 2000 the authorities of the split Moldovan republic, 40% of whose population holds a dual citizenship status of some sort, retaliated in despair to what they saw as an infringement on the sovereignty of Moldova and passed a citizenship reform that mandated the denaturalization of holders of dual citizenship unless they had acquired that status through mixed marriages.

Although the application of the law had been minimal until its eventual revocation in 2003, the story of its adoption is a telling indication of the inter-state tensions created by the use of dual citizenship towards explicitly nationalist-revisionist purposes by Romania. In the light of the use of dual citizenship by Romania to further a revisionist agenda, it is hardly surprising that Romania would be extremely sensitive, or even fearful, about the Hungarian offer of external citizenship to Hungarians in Romania, suspecting Hungary of intentions similar to those informing Romanian policies towards Moldova.

Paradoxically, the expansion of the European Union (EU) into the East-Central European region also raised the political

---

Ethnic Hungarians in Various European Countries, 2004

Hungary	9,967,000
Romania	1,431,000
Slovakia	560,000
Serbia	300,000
Ukraine	150,000
Germany	120,000
United Kingdom	80,000
Russia	76,000
Austria	40,000
Croatia	16,000

TAKEN FROM: Statistics compiled by editor.

---

stakes involved in the institution of non-resident dual citizenship. When, in 1992 Germany offered German citizenship to Silesian Germans living in Poland, a part of the population of Poland had received the benefits of European citizenship ahead of their ethnically Polish counterparts living in the same state who had to wait over a decade to acquire the same status. Were Hungary to offer non-resident dual citizenship to Hungarians in neighboring states, Hungarians in those states would become EU citizens ahead of their counterparts belonging to the majority nation. (With the exception of Hungarians in Slovakia and Slovenia, that joined the EU together with Hungary in 2004). The Hungarian case is not altogether unique in Europe: Albanian misgivings about creating a privileged "European" minority within a majority nation that is not part of the EU have led to pressures on Greece to surrender its plans to offer non-resident dual citizenship to the Greek minority in Albania.

Reactions to the Initiative Were Diverse

Political debates on the referendum initiative were tremendously polarized. In 2003, the initiative to call a referendum had not come from Hungarian parliamentary parties, but an organization not well integrated into Hungarian politics, the World Federation of Hungarians comprising members from among transborder Hungarians as well as from among the Hungarian diaspora all over the world. . . .

Initially, mainstream Hungarian parties on all sides reacted very cautiously to the initiative, along with the more moderate leaders of transborder minorities. Minority leaders were especially worried about the possibility of a negative outcome to a referendum, which, in their view, could do serious harm to minority Hungarians. Miklós Kovács, chairman of the Cultural Association of Ukrainian Hungarians, for instance, branded the referendum initiative the action of a "marginalized swindler", and other minority leaders, such as József Kasza of Serbia were also skeptical. Within Hungary itself, even those parties of the right that, a few months later came out in support of the referendum, remained conspicuously passive at the beginning.

An 81% majority of the Hungarian electorate either stayed away from the voting, or voted against the creation of non-resident dual citizenship.

Besides the anticipation of failure, the other reason for the initial passivity of rightist parties may be explained by the explicit commitment, made only two years earlier, in 2001, by the Orbán government to the European Council (EC) on the occasion of the EC's investigation of the status law [designed to provide some form of state-membership for transborder Hungarians without the creation of dual citizenship], that Hungary had no intention of extrapolating citizenship rights from the status law which, as they said, was in fact based on the "rejection of dual citizenship" for kin minorities. As the position paper of the Orbán government submitted to the Venice Commission in 2001 stated:

In fact, the Act [status law] recognizes that Hungarians abroad are citizens of the relevant states and clearly rejects the idea that the self-identification as Hungarians can be based on dual citizenship. Hungarian assistance to Hungarians abroad has always been and will continue to be carried out according to the practice of other European states, taking European norms into consideration in good faith and giving due attention to the spirit of cooperation between neighboring states. In the expression of its kin-state role, Hungary has always acknowledged that it has no citizen-like relationship whatsoever with Hungarians living in the neighboring countries when dealing with them.

After a few months however, the mainstream right-wing parties (FIDESZ and MDF) along with the President of the Republic eventually declared their support for the referendum, while the socialists and liberals openly turned against it. What followed was an agitated, occasionally hysterical, campaign leading up to the referendum that fulfilled the prophecy of its own failure by turning out as invalid on account of the low number of participants. This then, points to a third feature of the Hungarian story, namely that an 81% majority of the Hungarian electorate either stayed away from the voting, or voted against the creation of non-resident dual citizenship for transborder Hungarians. Among those who cast their ballots, amounting to 37.67% of the electorate, 51.57% voted in favor of the reform, 48.43% against.

The United States Needs to Better Assimilate Immigrants into the National Culture

Stanley Renshon

In the following viewpoint, the author examines the growing detachment of immigrants from the core values and ideals of the United States. The author insists that migrants to the United States need to be encouraged to form various bonds, including emotional and psychological attachments, to their new country. He also criticizes contemporary plans to reform immigration policy in the United States. Stanley Renshon is a scholar and the author of numerous books, including The 50% American: Immigration and National Identity in an Age of Terror.

As you read, consider the following questions:

1. According to the viewpoint's estimate, how many illegal immigrants live in the United States?

2. According to the viewpoint, what traits do both liberals and conservatives agree unite most Americans?

3. What were the main recommendations of the Chicago Council on Foreign Relations 2004 proposal on immigration?

Stanley Renshon, "Becoming American: The Hidden Core of the Immigration Debate," *Backgrounder: Center for Immigration Studies*, January 2007. www.cis.org. Reproduced by permission.

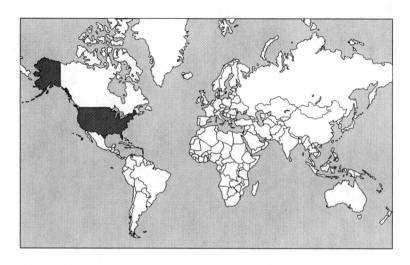

W hat is America's central, core immigration issue? It is this: How is it possible to integrate the almost 1 million new legal immigrants who arrive here each year, on average, into the American national community? How do we help them to feel more at home here, while at the same time developing the emotional attachments that will truly help them think of themselves as more American than otherwise? Before the United States adds 12 million illegal immigrants and their families to our citizenship rolls, stimulates the inevitable yearly increase in illegal aliens who will wish to be strategically placed for the next "status adjustment," and adds them to the already record-breaking numbers of legal immigrants who arrive each year, it should seriously consider the "attachment gap."

That gap is the result of centrifugal forces that have buffeted emotional attachments to the American national community by immigrants and Americans alike over the past four-plus decades. Domestically, multiculturalism has sought to substitute ethnic and racial attachments for national ones, while international cosmopolitans seek to transcend what they see as narrow and suspect nationalistic connections to the American community with international ties, including encouraging new immigrant ties to their "home" countries. All of this has unfolded as America's major cultural, political, and social institutions and practices have been under relentless pressure during our decades-long culture wars.

The focus on the emotional attachment and psychological integration of both new immigrants and those who are already American citizens into the American national community is, paradoxically, both fundamental and novel. Immigration is a policy area that has been dominated by economic arguments. Do immigrants pull their own economic weight? Do they use more economic resources than they contribute? Do they depress wages for working-class Americans? The degree of emotional attachment that immigrants feel toward their new country is hardly mentioned and never measured. Instead, we rely on surrogate measures like self-reports on English language faculty (which focus on speaking, not reading or writing), education, or home ownership. Caution is merited on all these substitute measures since few like to publicly admit their language limitations, education is not synonymous with national attachment as even a casual perusal of informed punditry will reveal, and owning a house is not the same as loving your country.

The immigration debate also has had its share of hyper-charged political rhetoric. Is helping immigrants to become attached to their new country a form of racism and cultural condescension? Are people who voice any concerns about immigration policy "anti-immigrant?" Facilitating the psychological attachment of immigrants and Americans alike to their country is too important an issue to allow it to be sidetracked by baseless accusations.

The Emotional Underpinnings of American Life

Emotional attachment to the American national community is the foundation of U.S. citizenship, this country's institutions, its way of life, and, in the wake of 9/11 [September 11, 2001 terrorist attacks in the U.S.], a matter of national security. Liberals and conservatives alike believe that a commitment to the American ideals of democracy and justice are what unites us. According to the Manhattan Institute's Tamar Jacoby, "every schoolchild knows we are a unique nation not by blood or ancestry, but by a set of shared ideas." Or again, what holds America together? "The ineluctable common core," Jacoby says, "is a set of ideas about how the American people ought to govern themselves."

Patriotism is much more complex than the adages 'my country right or wrong' or 'dissent is the highest form of patriotism.'

The political theorist Michael Walker has argued that it is citizenship and the fact that it is easy to become an American that binds us together. It is possible, of course, to have the rights of a citizen but to feel little emotional attachment to the country that provides them. This is one reason why a "guestworker" program that allows foreign workers to focus on higher paychecks that can be sent "home," takes American immigration policy in the wrong direction. In such cases citizenship is primarily instrumental, sought for the advantages it confers. Yet a community requires more than instrumental membership and a "what's in it for me?" calculus to function and prosper. Emotional attachments provide a community with the psychological resources to weather disappointments and disagreements and to help maintain a community's resolve in the face of historic dangers. Emotional attachment and identification are the mechanisms that underlie sacrifice, empathy, and service.

Citizenship without emotional attachment is the civic equivalent of a one-night stand. The power of the American Creed itself rests on a more basic psychological foundation. That foundation is the set of emotional attachments that often are disparaged and very misunderstood. The bonding

Assimilation Is a Two-Way Street

When it comes to American English—as the American journalist H.L. Mencken understood perfectly—its resourcefulness depends on the invigorating presence of immigrants arriving to the nation from every corner of the world. If the country performs its functions properly, those immigrants, in a relatively short period of time, will acquire enough English-language skills to become part of the social mosaic. But their assimilation is never a one-way street. As immigrants become Americans, the United States is altered too by their presence. This interchange is particularly recognizable at the level of language. Just as the Irish, Scandinavian, and Jewish newcomers became fluent speakers, so did the nation's tongue incorporate voices, expressions, syntactical patterns, and other verbal dexterities they brought along with them. And the rest of the population embraced those elements.

Ilan Stavans, "Change Is Gonna Do Ya Good," Dynamic English, U.S. Department of State, August 2007. http://usinfo.state.gov.

mechanisms through which "pluribus" becomes "unum" are the diverse emotional attachments that are ordinarily summarized by the term "patriotism."

Commitment to the United States

Patriotism is much more complex than the adages "my country right or wrong" or "dissent is the highest form of patriotism." And, contrary to the widely misquoted and misunderstood aphorism of Samuel Johnson, patriotism is not the "last resort of scoundrels," but an absolutely essential part of emotional bonding between Americans and their country. His oft-repeated quote referred only to those who misused the public trust, not to the virtues of patriotism. Johnson's real,

153

less reported, sentiment was that, "no man can deserve a seat in parliament who is not a patriot."

I understand patriotism or national attachment to include a warmth and affection for, an appreciation of, a justifiable but not excessive pride in, and a commitment and responsibility to the United States, its institutions, its way of life and aspirations, and its citizens. These attachments define the basis of our identification as Americans. We don't often think about it except when events like 9/11 remind us that our attachments to this country are profound and much deeper than simply believing that democracy is the best form of government. And they are much more extensive and nuanced than the caricature of lazy patriotism, summed up by the phrase "my country right or wrong."

The success of American democracy and its cultural and political institutions has always depended on these kinds of emotional connections. Yet over the past four-plus decades those attachments have been profoundly challenged, and in many ways weakened, by domestic and international developments. Within the United States, decades of cultural warfare over everything from the nature of families to civics curriculums have weakened America's primary social, political, and cultural institutions. At the same time, multiculturalism has successfully championed the primacy of racial and ethnic identities over more national attachments. Internationally, the ease of global movements of information and people have allowed immigrants and citizens alike to be in much closer touch with their "home" countries—and allowed their home countries to be more in touch with them, primarily for self-interested reasons.

The Country's Psychological Glue

New and old immigrants have understandable attachments to their countries of origin. The question is: How can the United States facilitate attachments to *this* country? The answer to that question does not concern new immigrants alone. These are American national community issues. Both old citizens and new immigrants have an important stake in increasing the extensiveness and depth of attachments to the American national community. And of course, the government, representing all Americans, has a critical role to play in helping to foster American national identity and attachment—a role it has so far declined to play.

If national attachments are the psychological glue that holds this country together, how is it possible to help develop and consolidate these feelings? Certainly no laws can mandate them. Nor can we halt or reverse the march of technology and international connectedness. The truth is that such feelings can only develop out of experiences that foster them. The question is whether we can help put into place experiences that do just that. . . .

In the years since the Jordan Commission report, the United States has demonstrated that it still is not serious about helping immigrants become Americans.

Each immigrant and citizen will have to find his or her own entry into the vast array of ways to be and live life as an American. There are a million stories in the big city, as the old television tag line began, or to update it, 300 million American stories and counting.

Finding points of attachment between Americans, old and new, and this country's history, institutions, and traditions so that immigrants can see how their lives and that of the country intersect provides one strong basis for emotional attachment and the development of an American identity. Government, as well as private and civic organizations at all levels, has an important, helping role to play in this process.

Psychological Integration Policies

Immigration policy reform proposals are not new. The Center for Immigration Studies' report, "Blueprint for an Ideal Immigration Policy," draws recommendations from across the political spectrum. For example, the authors suggest diversifying the immigrant stream, looking more closely at the issue of family preferences, and examining immigrant work programs as a method of increasing flexibility. These, and similar proposals, seem useful. However, they will not be my focus here. Instead I will focus on the particular question of emotionally integrating new immigrants and citizens alike into the American national community.

That concern is not new. Barbara Jordan and the U.S. Commission on Immigration Reform used very strong and direct language to underscore the point that Americanization was not a dirty word and that it was, in fact, a key element of successfully integrating new immigrants into the American national community. The Commission's report to Congress, "Becoming an American: Immigration and Immigrant Policy," is an overlooked treasure of sensible ideas. Regretfully, little has been done to implement the Jordan Commission's important insights. A 2004 study and policy proposals sponsored by the Chicago Council on Foreign Relations contain a few useful suggestions on this issue which parallel the Jordan Commission suggestions of a decade earlier: to develop federal, state, local, and civic partnerships to help immigrants and to ensure that they learn English. Yet they also add some new ideas that are less central: streamlining and speeding up naturalization, disabusing American "misperceptions" about immigrants, and giving health insurance benefits to new immigrants. These suggestions do not seem to get to the heart of the issues.

In the years since the Jordan Commission report, the United States has demonstrated that it still is not serious about helping immigrants become Americans. Nor has much thought been given to how we can help Americans themselves consolidate their connections with their home country. The two are certainly related. If Americans have difficulty understanding and appreciating their country, how can we expect new immigrants to fare much better? In the post-9/11 age of catastrophic terrorism, this is a dangerous gap. The failure to affirmatively act in this matter is not primarily the result of public indifference; there is overwhelming support among Americans for integrating immigrants into American life. Indeed, what upsets Americans most about immigration, aside from the continuing surge of illegal immigration, is the sense that the traditional expectation of immigrant integration into the American national communities is no longer valued by some or expected by many—among them our political leaders.

Not all of the suggestions made about reforming immigration policy further the integration of new immigrants. Some feel that the burdens of becoming an American citizen are already too heavy, and they propose to lighten them. Some want to lessen, or do away with, the requirement that immigrants learn English. Some want to include illegal aliens in a new general amnesty. And some want to do away with the renunciation clause in the Naturalization Oath, arguing that you cannot legislate feelings. These suggestions, for what amount to the immigrant citizenship version of automobile EZ passes for toll collection, do not seem designed to foster attachment. On the contrary, they promise to further fracture the American national community and the feelings of emotional connection that underlie it.

Periodical Bibliography

The following articles have been selected to supplement the diverse views presented in this chapter.

Don Belt	"Europe's Big Gamble," *National Geographic*, May 2004.
Richard Brookhiser	"America's Fear of Outsiders," *Time*, May 31, 2007.
Eduardo Cue	"The New Faces of Spain," *U.S. News & World Report*, April 28, 2008.
Walter Ellis	"Welcome to the United States of Latin America," *Times Higher Education Supplement*, June 18, 2004.
Daniel Faas	"Youth, Europe and the Nation: The Political Knowledge, Interests and Identities of the New Generation of European Youth," *Journal of Youth Studies*, May 2007.
Peter Honey	"African Immigrants: Fewer Than Was Thought," *Financial Mail*, February 16, 2007.
Tim Johnston	"Australians Debating Immigration and National Identity," *International Herald Tribune*, January 28, 2007.
Eleonore Kofman	"Citizenship, Migration and the Reassertion of National Identity," *Citizenship Studies*, November 2005.
Theodora Lam and Brenda S. A. Yeoh	"Negotiating 'Home' and 'National Identity:' Chinese-Malaysian Transmigrants in Singapore," *Asia Pacific Viewpoint*, August 2004.
Lawrence Lindsey	"Can Immigration Reform Work?" *Weekly Standard*, May 22, 2006.
Quadrant Magazine	"Immigration and Its Discontents," September 2004.

GLOBALVIEWPOINTS

CHAPTER 4

Immigration and National Security

The United Kingdom's Immigration and Asylum Practices Unfairly Detain Immigrants

Christine Bacon

In the following viewpoint, the author argues against the growing trend in the United Kingdom for private prisons to house detained immigrants. She points out that criminals in the United Kingdom have extensive civil liberties, but immigrants face various forms of repression and may be detained for lengthy periods of time. Bacon is an activist for refugee rights. Formerly, she worked with the European Council on Refugees and Exiles in London.

As you read, consider the following questions:

1. According to the viewpoint, which groups in the United Kingdom are most opposed to the privatization of prisons?

2. In the United Kingdom, are the immigration agencies subject to the same oversight as the criminal justice system?

3. According to the viewpoint, do private prison companies seek to increase or decrease the number of immigrant detainees?

Christine Bacon, "The Evolution of Immigration Detention in the UK: The Involvement of Private Prison Companies," *Refugee Studies Centre Working Paper 27*, September 2005. www.rsc.ox.ac.uk. Reproduced by permission.

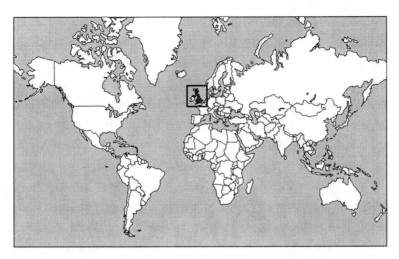

During the course of the last decade, asylum has become one of the most salient political issues in the UK [United Kingdom]. The years 1993–2004 have seen no less than five major pieces of asylum-focused legislation enacted, where previously none had existed. This increasingly restrictive and somewhat impenetrable accumulation of laws and regulations has developed in conjunction with a broad effort to control asylum numbers and 'root out abuse'. Perhaps one of the most disturbing features of the armoury of measures employed in relation to the achievement of these aims has been the administrative and often prolonged detention of asylum seekers. Despite the government's assurance that detention is used only as a 'last resort', a growing number of asylum seekers, who are not suspected of or charged with any offence, are routinely detained in purpose-built detention centres and criminal prisons throughout the UK. This use of detention has expanded rapidly, from a capacity of 250 places in 1993 to the present capacity for 2,644 persons.

The Debate over Immigration Detention

People concerned with immigration detention have tended to see it as an issue mainly involving government policy makers, detainees and immigration officers, but have neglected one of the key players, namely the private companies contracted to run the centres. These companies could arguably be seen as the 'missing link' in what appears to be a more and more anomalous practice, and may provide further insight into how and why the regime has managed to maintain itself over time. While this thesis does not suggest that the involvement of private companies constitutes an overarching or driving explanation for the evolution of the detention regime or the rise of harsher practices over time, it offers a complementary explanation which seeks to demonstrate that the growth of the detention regime is not based solely on ever-restrictive asylum laws and policies. Its growth can also be attributed to the involvement private contractors, whose logic of response to asylum seekers has very little to do with the logic of the government's response, concerned as they are with winning and maintaining contracts and keeping their facilities full.

A strict regime of time limits is imposed on the detention of criminal arrestees, while an immigration detainee can be detained for an indefinite period.

The privatisation of prisons in the UK and elsewhere remains controversial. Along with a sceptical public, penal reformers and criminologists, in particular, remain deeply opposed to the movement and this interest has yielded a large volume of scholarly contributions. The privatisation of immigration detention centres, however, has tended only to receive a cursory glance in relevant debates and scholarly analyses. This omission is puzzling, given that the companies with a large stake in private prisons are the very same as those who have a large stake in privately run immigration detention centres. Malcolm Feeley points to a similar omission when he notes that private prisons in the US [United States] continue to attract controversy, but 'private facilities for juveniles go virtually unnoticed, although they house half, or more, juveniles in custody in the United States.'

The companies in question see their involvement in immigration detention as being firmly within the penal sphere. One company, for example, lists immigration contracts under its 'justice' sector and has called its involvement in immigration detention a 'natural extension' to its custodial work. Immigration detention has been identified as the next, highly profitable frontier for the growing incarceration sector in recent years and the executives employed to win contracts in custodial services bid for prisons and immigration detention contracts alike. Contracts with the Immigration and Nationality Directorate of the Home Office (IND) provide the private contractor with a fee per inmate per day and are extremely lucrative. In fact, United Kingdom Detention Services (UKDS) reported a turnover of £12.18 million for its operation at Harmondsworth immigration detention centre for the year ended 31 August 2002, not much less than its turnover for its Forest Bank prison operation at £13.6 million. Moreover, a great deal more immigration detention centres are managed by the private sector than are prisons. Australia is an extreme case, in which all of the detention estate is in private hands, but the UK is not far behind, with seven of the ten centres being run by the private sector. This compares to around ten per cent of prisons.

Inequality Among Prisoners

Furthermore, in comparison to the volume of legislation regulating private prisons and prison escorts, there is very little for immigration detention centres and the immigration escort sector. Immigration detainees are stripped of many of the legal safeguards suspected criminals are entitled to. At police stations, for example, a strict regime of time limits is imposed on the detention of criminal arrestees, while an immigration detainee can be detained for an indefinite period. After a maximum of 24 hours, a criminal suspect must be released or charged unless continued detention is authorized by an officer of at least the rank of superintendent and the suspect is under arrest in connection with a serious arrestable offence. The officer must have grounds to believe that detention is still necessary to secure, preserve or obtain evidence relating to the offence and that the investigation is conducted expeditiously. In any event, no detention without charge is permitted after 96 hours. There is also a presumption in favour of release in criminal bail hearings and full access to legal assistance and full appeal rights. One of the major concerns about private prison operations is the inherent lack of transparency and accountability. As the IND is not part of the criminal justice system, there is even more scope for corporations to resist scrutiny and an environment of diminished legal oversight has come to characterise the asylum and detention system.

It has been suggested that the relative lack of public interest in the plight of asylum seekers and non-citizens and the fact that they enjoy fewer and narrower legal protections has made it possible to use the detention of aliens as an experimental ground for testing the effectiveness of privatisation in this field. However, this cannot fully explain the lack of interest in this area. [J.] Vagg points out that before the decision was made to contract out the first prison to private sector management, a large number of juvenile detention centres and probation hostels in Britain were actually run by private or voluntary agencies without attracting much concern. A more plausible explanation as to the lack of academic and public interest in this phenomenon is perhaps linked to the perception of immigration detention as 'administrative' rather than 'punitive'. Moreover, the fact that private management of the centres has become such an integral and essential part of the UK's immigration detention system has perhaps allowed its private nature to be practically invisible, even to those

Problems with a Private Prison

The Home Office has pledged to review the management of a privately run prison where an investigation by Guardian Films and the BBC [British Broadcasting Company]uncovered routine bullying of staff by prisoners at the jail.

A reporter working undercover as a prison officer at the troubled Rye Hill jail found widespread intimidation of staff and incidents where diligent custody officers were urged to "back off" by senior colleagues for fear of upsetting inmates. . . .

The Jail had already been heavily criticised by inspectors over the murder of an inmate and the "avoidable" suicides of prisoners.

Matt Weaver, "Home Office Promises Review After Prison Exposè"
The Guardian, April 16, 2007. www.guardian.co.uk.

working in the area. This may explain why private prisons, being only a small part of the system, still manage to attract considerable controversy.

The Private Interests of Private Prisons

It would seem that any argument seeking to question the development and use of private prison operators would be strengthened by the case of immigration detention. While agreeing with David Garland, who has argued that penal policy is the outcome of a 'large number of conflicting forces' and it is ultimately impossible to identify and analyse the full range of 'swarming circumstances' that work to shape penal developments, detailed studies on private interests in immigration detention can lead to a fuller understanding of the determinants of detention policy in the UK. Refugee scholars have largely focused on legal, policy and human rights concerns when writing about immigration detention and have tended not to investigate the deeper structural factors and interests at play. These scholars, along with practitioners and advocates in the field, should be very concerned about mixing corporate business practice where private profit is the driving force, with the detention of asylum seekers and non-citizens, especially given that asylum applications in the UK have decreased significantly in recent years, while the use of immigration detention continues to expand. In this context, it would seem necessary to question a system in which private companies have a vested interest in keeping the immigration detention population as high as possible. . . .

[T]he privatisation of immigration detention centers is open to criticism on a number of levels, and can be directly linked to the growth of the detention estate, the willingness to detain despite clear principles and rules limiting its use, the secrecy and lack of accountability inherent in immigration detention, and in some respects, the move towards increasingly harsh detention policy and practice. It concludes that the implications of privatization of immigration detention centers are of grave concern and that at the very least, boundaries as to the extent of private involvement and the capacity of detention space, should be clearly defined. This is especially significant when considering the detention of asylum seekers, who should be detained only as a 'last resort'.

Moroccan Migration Creates Security Concerns in Spain

Lisa Abend and Geoff Pingree

In the following viewpoint, the authors explore emigration from Morocco to Europe, mainly Spain. They examine how the loss of talented Moroccans, including doctors and other professionals, undermines the country's economic security. They also explore the efforts by Spain to curb illegal immigration, including policy that would return illegal immigrants to Morocco within twenty-four hours. Lisa Abend and Geoff Pingree are both correspondents for The Christian Science Monitor.

As you read, consider the following questions:

1. What is Morocco's unemployment rate? How does it compare with Spain's unemployment rate?
2. According to the viewpoint, how much does it cost to emigrate from Morocco to Spain?
3. How does Spain treat illegal immigrants who are minors differently than they do the adults?

Omar was 17 when he stole aboard a freight truck in Tangier, Morocco. Determined to find a different life, he burrowed into the truck's cargo—piles of women's underwear—to hide.

Lisa Abend and Geoff Pingree, "Morocco's Biggest European Export: People—Thousands Flood Spain Annually, Fueling the Economy and Raising Security Concerns," *The Christian Science Monitor*, September 29, 2005. Reproduced by permission from Christian Science Monitor, (www.csmonitor.com).

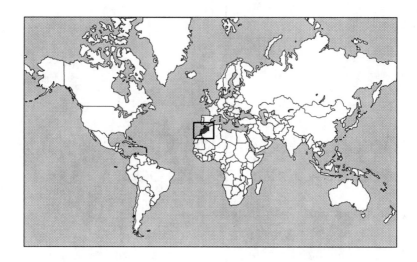

Soon, he discovered another boy, also seeking passage out of Morocco, hiding there. As the truck boarded the ferry to cross the straits of Gibraltar, border police caught that young man. Omar went undetected. Within hours he was in Murcia, where he joined the hundreds of thousands of Moroccans who have immigrated illegally to Spain.

Spain is the primary entryway to Europe for the approximately 30,000 Moroccans who emigrate each year.

Just eight watery miles from Tangier, Spain is the primary entryway to Europe for the approximately 30,000 Moroccans who emigrate each year. Around 4 million Moroccans live abroad—roughly 12 percent of the country's population. Spain is home to Europe's second largest Moroccan community.

Moroccan Disparities

The reasons for this exodus, says Mehdi Lahlou, a professor of economics at Rabat's National Institute of Statistics and Economics, are readily apparent: poverty and unemployment. "Thirty years ago, when the economic levels of Spain and Morocco were the same, Moroccans didn't emigrate there," says Mr. Lahlou. "But now the economic difference between Spain and Morocco is 20 to 1."

Morocco's gross national product [GNP] per inhabitant is just $3,600—barely a sixth of Spain's. Its unemployment rate, nearly 20 percent in urban areas, is more than twice that of its northern neighbor. And differences in health care and social opportunities echo the countries' economic gap: Moroccans, on average, live 10 years less than Spaniards, and barely half can read, while 97 percent of Spaniards are literate.

For Spain, Morocco's emigrant tide is both boon and threat. It bolsters the economy by bringing countless workers who will take jobs Spaniards no longer want, but it also raises concerns within local Spanish communities about security, unemployment, and social stability.

Despite the perception in Spain that Moroccan immigrants tend to be impoverished illiterates prone to crime, Moroccans who emigrate are not that country's most destitute citizens. "It costs 5,000 or 6,000 euros to emigrate," says Lahlou, "so they tend to come from the mid-skilled classes, not from the poorest."

More than anything else, it is a perceived lack of opportunity that encourages citizens to leave their country. In his recent film, "Tarfaya," Moroccan director Daoud Aoulad Syad chronicled one girl's perilous attempts to gain illegal passage to the Canary Islands. "Most of the people in Tarfaya dream of being somewhere else. That's why they all have satellite dishes. They're not watching Moroccan TV, they're watching French and Spanish, aspiring to be somewhere else," says Mr. Syad.

Emigration's Economic Dilemma

The fact that so many Moroccans dream of leaving significantly threatens Morocco's economic development, social well-being, and political stability. "Every year Morocco loses 2 to 3 percent of its GNP to brain drain," says Lahlou. "Every year we lose between 3,000 and 5,000 professors, doctors, and engineers annually."

This loss means fewer well-educated, ambitious citizens who could help lead their country. But there is an irony here, for if through emigration Morocco loses capital in some forms, it gains it through the money its emigrants send back to their families. Indeed, the International Monetary Fund reports that a full 9 percent of Morocco's GNP comes from remittances—a percentage far greater than the 1.66 percent sent home by Mexicans working in the US [United States].

This dilemma may help explain why the Moroccan government can seem ambivalent about its policy on illegal emigration. "We don't have oil," says Nouzha Chekrouni, Minister for Moroccans Living Abroad. "Our greatest resource, our most valuable export, is our human potential. Europe needs our emigrants."

At the insistence of many European countries, however, Morocco has stepped up efforts to control what it terms "clandestine emigration." Chakri Draiss, Morocco's civil governor in Laayoune, notes that in his region alone, 4,000 illegal emigrants were captured in the first six months of the year [2005]. "We also created mixed patrols with the Spanish Civil Guard so that the Spanish can see our efforts."

Ms. Chekrouni, however, sees economic development as the key to curbing illegal emigration, and she says that Europe's crackdown is counter-productive. "Security is not the only answer," she says. "It only increases the efforts of the mafia who traffic in immigrants."

The Spanish Solution

For its part, Spain recently adopted a policy of returning to Morocco within 24 hours all apprehended illegal immigrants.

Moroccan Authorities Do Little to Prevent Illegal Migration to Spain

The number of stowaways hiding in lorries [in Tangier, Morocco, prior to smuggling themselves to Spain] has increased dramatically.

"The situation is really getting worse and worse, it's desperate. We're finding people hidden in our lorries every single week now," says Laetitia Banzet [of the British logistics company Tibbett and Britten].

Like many transport companies in Tangier she has little faith in the Moroccan police authorities and employs her own security staff to protect drivers and lorries from gangs of migrants.

Tamsin Smith, "Policing Spain's Southern Coast,"
BBC News, May 2004. http://news.bbc.co.uk.

But since the policy applies to adults only—minors can stay—the number of Moroccan immigrant minors in Spain has skyrocketed.

On his first day in Spain, Omar was picked up by a lawyer who drove him to an immigrant asylum center. Eventually he landed at La Merced, a center in Madrid supported by a religious order and run by Father Perez, who ensures the home's residents—immigrants under 18—learn Spanish, acquire vocational skills, and achieve the ability to navigate Spanish culture.

Today, Omar (who didn't want his last name published) has residency papers and works as a gardener. He is not wholly enamored of his job and hopes one day to have his own business. Now 21, he appreciates the freedoms that Spain offers—

especially when it comes to going out at night and meeting girls. But he misses his family, and he often wonders if he made the right choice.

"If I knew then what I know now," he says wistfully, "I wouldn't have come. I would have stayed there and finished my studies."

Australia Changed Its Illegal Immigration Policy in Response to International Criticism

Stephen de Tarczynski

In the following viewpoint, the author examines changes to Australia's immigration policy. Previously, Australia transported illegal immigrants it apprehended to offshore islands to prevent them from staying on the country's mainland. In some cases, the detained immigrants spent years on the islands before their cases were resolved. However, following a change in government after the 2007 elections, revisions to the policy were undertaken and many of those held in detention were released. De Tarczynski is an Australian writer and journalist.

As you read, consider the following questions:

1. What is the Australian "Pacific Solution"?
2. According to the viewpoint, how did Australia's immigrant detention policy conflict with international law?
3. How did the "Pacific Solution" affect Australia's international reputation, according to the viewpoint?

While advocates of asylum seekers have supported the new Australian government's plan to wind down part of the so-called 'Pacific Solution' for processing claims for asylum, they argue that the government should go further.

Stephen de Tarczynski, "Rights Australia: 'Pacific Solution' for Boat People Rolled Back," IPS, January 4, 2008. http://ipsnews.net. Reproduced by permission.

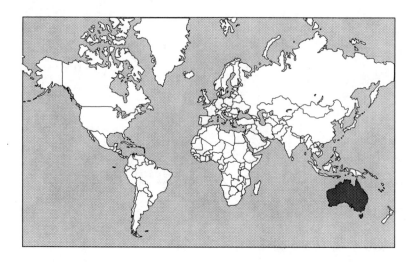

"I think the reaction of the Refugee Council and many other groups is that the Pacific Solution was a completely unnecessary and dehumanising way of responding to the situation of people arriving by boat and seeking asylum in Australia," says Paul Power, chief of the Refugee Council of Australia (RCOA), who welcomed the Rudd government's announcement to scale back the controversial program.

Australia enacted laws in 2001 which removed some offshore territories—including the Cocos Islands and Ashmore Reef—from the country's migration zone in an attempt to deter refugees from seeking a safe haven.

Hope for Detainees

The 'Pacific Solution' was introduced under the Howard Government in 2001 in order to stem what it regarded as an influx of illegal arrivals to Australia by boat. The 'solution' involved sending asylum seekers to offshore detention centres—where people would sometimes languish for years—on the tiny Pacific island nation of Nauru and on Papua New Guinea's Manus Island.

Under the deal, the Pacific nations involved are believed to have received financial aid from Australia, which also covered all costs for the running of the camps.

Kon Karapanagiotidis, chief of the Asylum Seeker Resource Centre (ACRC)—a provider of aid, advocacy and health services to asylum seekers—describes the 'Pacific Solution' as "appalling".

"The human consequence and damage caused to all those people that have rotted away on those little island prison camps; it's one of the most disgusting things I've ever seen done in Australian politics," Karapanagiotidis told IPS [Inter Press Service News Agency].

During the campaign for November's [2007] federal election, Kevin Rudd's Labour Party pledged to bring an end to the 'Pacific Solutions'. . . . [In December 2007], Immigration Minister, Chris Evans, announced that the seven Burmese asylum seekers being held in a camp in Nauru would be granted refugee status, thereby allowing them to be settled in Australia.

The detention centre on Manus Island is already empty, yet some 80 Sri Lankan asylum seekers remain on Nauru. The government says that it intends to resolve their cases quickly.

With the imminent closure of these offshore detention centres, mainstream Australian media has been quick to announce the end of the 'Pacific Solution'. But while the government has signalled the beginning of the end for the system of detaining asylum seekers in foreign countries, other aspects of the 'Pacific Solution' remain.

As part of the 'solution', Australia enacted laws in 2001 which removed some offshore territories—including the Cocos Islands and Ashmore Reef—from the country's migration zone in an attempt to deter refugees from seeking a safe haven in the world's largest island.

Another Blow for Asylum Seekers

This excising of Australia's migration zone meant that asylum seekers who landed in these excised territories lost rights that they would otherwise have been entitled to. The laws meant that asylum seekers could not automatically apply for refugee status and enabled Australia to move them to a third country while their applications were processed.

These excised migration zones will remain under the Rudd Government, but a spokesman for Minister Evans told IPS . . . that the government will review this in 2008.

Karapanagiotidis argues that the excising of Australia's migration zone was part of an attempt to undermine the refugee convention—a United Nations agreement setting out the rights of refugees and the responsibilities of countries providing asylum to those seeking protection—charge that the Howard government consistently denied.

"The idea of basically trying to circumvent and destroy the refugee convention (and) undermine one of the most critical human rights treaties on the face of the earth, all for political expediency and for self-interest is base politics at its worst," says Karapanagiotidis.

Christmas Island—located in the Indian Ocean some 2600 kilometers northwest of Perth and 500 kilometers south of Jakarta—excised from the country's migration zone, was also used by the Howard Government as a detention centre for asylum seekers.

Despite telling IPS that the Rudd government is indeed ending the 'Pacific Solution', Evans' spokesman says that asylum seekers will still be detained on Christmas Island.

Karapanagiotidis argues that the government should reverse the excising of the migration zones that occurred under the Howard government and close the Christmas Island detention centre. "It's not good enough that they're doing away with the 'Pacific Solution' but not Christmas Island," he says.

The Costs of the Pacific Solution

So far the cost of the Pacific Solution is $500,000 per person to process fewer than 1,700 asylum seekers. And yet there's clear evidence that it's cheaper, more effective and humane to process asylum seekers here on the mainland. It makes no economic sense whatsoever to house a detainee offshore at a cost of $1,830 per day when it can be done here on mainland Australia for as little as $238 per day.

Oxfam Australia,
"Counting the Cost of Unaccountable Pacific Solution,"
September 3, 2007. www.oxfam.org.au.

"If we're committed to our refugee obligations under the treaty, that would involve doing away with excised borders and processing people onshore," Karapanagiotidis told IPS.

Paul Power says that the Refugee Council will also be advocating for the migration zones to be restored. Additionally, he believes that "one of the few things the Rudd government needs to look at doing is just calming down the shrill voices in the Australian population who see people seeking protection from persecution as somehow a threat."

Policy Recommendations

Both advocates want the new government to end the controversial mandatory detention of asylum seekers—a policy begun under the Paul Keating-led Labour government in 1992—but given the potential electoral fallout that such a policy change could generate, Karapanagiotidis is far from confident of a successful campaign.

"They're never going to do away with mandatory detention. I don't think any government is going to have the political courage to do that," he says.

Karapanagiotidis told IPS that he wants mandatory detention to be a last resort. "Unless there is a compelling public concern for our safety, let people out, do not detain them," he argues.

Power says the 'Pacific Solution' impacted negatively on Australia's reputation. "It was really sad that the politicians chose to focus on some of the world's most vulnerable people—people seeking protection from persecution and conflict—to create what they saw as political mileage," he told IPS.

Karapanagiotidis agrees, arguing that the 'solution' "did massive damage to our international standing". But he is hopeful that the Rudd government can bring about real change.

"They've been making the right sounds, but we need to now see some action to follow it through," he says.

Russian Fears of Immigration Are Exaggerated

Mikhail A. Alexseev and C. Richard Hofstetter

In the following viewpoint, the authors analyze the impact of Chinese immigration on Russian public opinion in the Far East. Of particular concern for many Russians is the imbalance between the Chinese and the Russian populations in the region. However, the authors find that many Russian fears are exaggerated and have not been substantiated. Mikhail A. Alexseev and C. Richard Hofstetter are both political science professors at San Diego State University. Alexseev's latest book is Immigration Phobia and the Security Dilemma: Russia, Europe, and the United States.

As you read, consider the following questions:

1. According to the viewpoint, what is the security dilemma?

2. What is "migration phobia," and how do the authors describe its impact on public opinion?

3. According to one estimate, how many Chinese are there for each Russian on the Chinese-Russian border?

Since the opening of the Sino-Soviet border in 1988, governors of Siberian and Russian Far Eastern territories, Russian federal government officials, and the media have been

Mikhail A. Alexseev, and C. Richard Hofstetter, "Russia, China, and the Immigration Security Dilemma," *Political Science Quarterly*, vol. 121, no. 1, Spring 2006, pp. 1–5, 7, 8. Reproduced by permission.

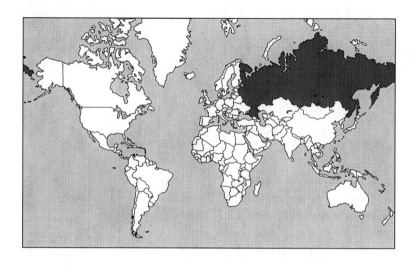

warning the Kremlin and the Russian public about "peaceful Chinese infiltration" and "Sinification" of the Russian Far East (RFE). In national polls conducted by the Levada Analytical Center, Russia's leading survey agency, the number of respondents who wanted to restrict the settlement of ethnic Chinese in Russia rose from 39 percent to 46 percent from 2004 to 2005. Resembling responses to migration in host societies from California to the suburbs of Paris—and nurturing premonitions that the French urban riots of late 2005 may repeat themselves at the juncture of Eurasia's two most powerful states—these dire warnings and exclusionist sentiments have been counterintuitive in several important respects. Migrants have been associated with threats to group and national security precisely where they are much needed to offset the decline of the working-age population to revitalize local economies. Moreover, hostility emerged despite the widely recognized willingness of migrants to work harder and for longer hours in lower-paid jobs than host populations do and to move where workers are scarcest. Alarmist reactions have also persisted regardless of the decline in illegal migration rates from the early 1990s to the present, and regardless of the fact that for over more than a decade, migration has not produced any sizeable Chinese ethnic enclaves in the RFE. Finally, the tenacity of anti-Chinese sentiments in the region has been impervious to the improvement of Sino-Russian relations in the 1990s—as marked by the settlement of border disputes, regular summit meetings, substantial arms trade, and a friendship treaty. These puzzles about the persistence of "yellow peril" alarmism in the RFE relate to a broader theoretical problem identified in a recent review of research on migration and conflict: "Whether migration heightens tensions . . . often depends on whether it is viewed as undermining national security or domestic harmony, but the process by which threats are constructed and by which boon is transformed into bane remains poorly understood and under-theorized." In this article, we develop a theoretical explanation of antimigrant alarmism and hostility by drawing on the security dilemma perspective, especially as it applies to relations among ethnic groups.

Perceptions and Misperceptions About the State of Security

At the heart of the security dilemma is a desire for self-preservation strongly associated with the absence or decline of central government authority. According to John Herz's original definition: "Whenever such anarchic society has existed—and it has existed in most periods of known history on some level—there has arisen what may be called the 'security dilemma' of men, or groups, or their leaders. Groups or individuals living in such a constellation must be, and usually are, concerned about their security from being attacked, subjected, dominated or annihilated by other groups and individuals." Thus, threats blown out of seemingly rational proportion would nevertheless have solid bases in social reality and human psychology. Regarding ethnic relations, the security dilemma refers to obsession with relative power "when proximate groups of people suddenly find themselves newly responsible for their own security." Emphasizing the critical role of perception and misperception during periods of uncertainty, the security dilemma provides an internally consistent and parsimonious explanation for precisely why fears may arise and become endemic, pervasive, irrational, symbolic, exaggerated, and potentially uncontrollable, even in the face of a stated commitment to peace and cooperation by all groups or states. In this sense, the security dilemma directly addresses the central theoretical puzzle of the present study—the emergence and persistence of what may be called "migration phobia," even when migration yields net economic benefits, when most migrants are temporary, and when intergovernmental relations between migrant-sending and -receiving states improve. And because the security dilemma logic has to do with competing interpretations of the nature, scale, and outcomes of migration, we define migration broadly as the movement of people—permanent or temporary—from one country or locality to another.

[The Russian Far East is] a case where no mass interethnic violence had occurred as a result of migration, yet where anti-migrant alarmism and hostility have been palpable.

The Security Dilemma Complex and Logic

As cross-border movement of ethnically heterogeneous groups, migration is one process that would make various groups proximate and potentially insecure. First, the very fact of migration could be perceived as a symptom of "borderlessness" and, hence, of declining state sovereignty and government authority. And by raising uncertainty about the future ethnic makeup of states (regardless of actual migration scale), migration would make incumbent ethnic groups more likely to view competition for power as key to their security. Second, ethnic incumbents could rarely be certain that temporary migrants would return home and would not settle down, bring in their relatives and friends, and claim jobs, resources, or territory (that is, "offense" is indistinguishable from "defense"). Histories of territorial claims and records of violent conflict between the migrants and the host populations would also decrease credibility of the migrants' intent. Third, migration often brings together ethnic populations who have a sense of distinct "groupness" and entrenched negative stereotypes—giving xenophobic politicians opportunities to manipulate ethnic mythologies in the struggle for power. Fourth, migration may engender economic rivalries and competition, activating the sense of economic vulnerability in host societies. The more intense these perceptions—the "security dilemma complex"—the more would one expect migration to engender fear and hostility despite efforts of all groups to assert their good will.

The Russian Far East population in the 1990s declined by almost 9 percent due to the prevalence of deaths over births and out-migration to European Russia.

However, Jack Snyder and Robert Jervis caution that the security dilemma is "a social situation with social and perceptual causes, not simply a fact of nature. None of the elements that fuel the security dilemma—neither anarchy, nor offensive advantages, nor expectations that others will defect—can be taken for granted as unproblematic givens." Actual or anticipated shifts in ethnic balance would not automatically harden into security dilemma situations, even in near-anarchical environments. Individual fears of ethnic "other" newcomers may differ widely in the same fear-producing environments. In two areas of the world in which interethnic security dilemma conditions have been most apparent—Africa and the former Soviet Union—violent conflict occurred in only a fraction of interethnic dyads.

Alarmism Exists Even Before Threats or Violence

Whereas previous research on the interethnic security dilemma has offered us increasingly sophisticated theoretical refinements, empirical studies have relied on descriptive case studies—in which mass violence had already occurred. However, such methodology is insufficient to address critical questions about the long-term social and psychological dynamics of ethnic conflict that concern us in this study: How do perceived shifts in ethnic population balances translate into fear and hostility toward ethnic "others" long before incendiary speeches are written and guns are fired? Do threat perceptions actually emerge among living, breathing human beings under structural conditions and leaders' behavior that one associates with the security dilemma as specified by theory? Under these same conditions, do some individuals find their futures more threatening than do others, and why? Which perceptions may mitigate fears? To address these questions—in a way previous studies could not do by design—we focus on the RFE as a case where no mass interethnic violence had occurred as a result of migration, yet where anti-migrant alarmism and hostility have been palpable. We analyze migration phobia with a hope to advance our understanding of the security dilemma logic, before governments actually break down and violence erupts. . . .

In the Russian Far East, widespread fears of "Sinification" (*kitaizatsiia*) emerged in the 1990s in a demographic and political context. . . . First, migrants arrived from a vastly more populated state, with migration, by its very occurrence, symbolizing the population disparity between Russia and China. In Primorskii Krai, 2.2 million Russians faced 38 million Chinese in one neighboring Heilongjiang province alone, with Russian scholars commonly estimating Heilongjiang's population at 70 million. Only about 7 million Russians in the late 1990s populated the entire Russian Far East—about 37 percent of Russia's territory, stretching from Lake Baikal to the Pacific Ocean and bordering China with over 1.2 billion people. Moreover, the Russian Far East population in the 1990s declined by almost 9 percent due to the prevalence of deaths over births and out-migration to European Russia.

Chinese Population Pressure

Implying the threatening nature of these population dispari-ties, Russian academics and policy analysts see them as result-ing in China's "demographic pressure" on Russia. By one esti-mate, this pressure amounts to 63,000 Chinese nationals per one Russian, per one kilometer of the Russian-Chinese border. Population density pressure was estimated at 380,000 Chinese per one Russian per one kilometer inside a one-kilometer band of the same border. The former Vice-Governor of Pri-morskii Krai, Vladimir Stegnii, also said he feared that by 2050, China's population growth would overextend that country's carrying capacity, necessitating territorial expansion to satisfy the need for water, air, and land. Assessing the effects of migration on Sino-Russian relations, Dmitry Trenin of the Moscow Carnegie Center argued that "even a relatively small number of Chinese immigrants would be enough to com-pletely upset the current ethnopolitical balance. . . . In those circumstances, the absence of clear and consistent immigra-tion policy practically guarantees the rise of interethnic ten-sions that could relatively easily escalate into an interstate conflict between Russia and China."

Russian Misperceptions and Exaggerated Estimates

What Trenin describes as a "demographic overhang" (*demograficheskii naves*) of China over the RFE casts a long and threatening shadow over perceptions of Chinese migra-tion. It is understandable in this context that even a small number of short-term Chinese migrants such as "shuttle trad-

Chinese Immigration May Lead to Violence in Russia

There are some 18 million ethnic Russians in Siberia; there are now about 300 million Chinese across the border in China's northern provinces.

As Russians leave the sparsely populated eastern territories in search of opportunities in the country's increasingly prosperous cities, waves of (mostly illegal) Chinese migrants are moving in. The trend is likely to intensify, feeding an anti-Chinese xenophobia that has existed in Russia for centuries. The risk of interethnic violence is bound to grow, complicating relations between the two governments.

Ian Bremmer "Should We Be Worried About Russia and China Ganging up on the West?" August 29, 2007. www.slate.com.

ers" (*chelnoki*) would serve as a powerful reminder of this demographic overhang to RFE residents and engender exaggerated estimates of migration scale among the latter. Indeed, perceptions that Chinese migrants would keep coming like a flood tide were widespread among respondents of the Primorskii 2000 survey. When asked what proportion of the Primorskii Krai population was Chinese, 46 percent of respondents (excluding the "don't knows") said that this proportion amounted to 10 to 20 percent (modal response). Looking five to ten years ahead, 41 percent of respondents said that the proportion of ethnic Chinese in Primorskii would grow to 20 to 40 percent, and another 20 percent said that it would reach 40 to 60 percent. (The actual number of Chinese migrants in Primorskii did not exceed 1 to 1.5 percent of the predominantly Slavic local population at the time).

Exaggerated assessments of migration scale would plausibly give rise to prospective fears that cross-border migration of an ethnically distinct group—however small and transient—would gradually increase demographic intermingling and create a de facto nation-bisecting interstate border. Once given to suspicion that migration might bring home the demographic overhang, residents in host communities may also find it plausible that, over time, migration would, as Stephen Van Evera put it, "entrap parts of nations within the boundaries of states dominated by other ethnic groups." Even in the absence of large permanent settlements, the security dilemma logic suggests that incumbent residents would become concerned that the prospective "truncated nation" or a "nested minority" (that is, the Chinese in Russia) would have incentive for expansionism. And to minimize the risk of "nested minorities" emerging in their territory, members of the "entrapping nation" (the Russians in the Far East), would then favor preemptive coercive and hostile action against cross-border migrants.

Periodical Bibliography

The following articles have been selected to supplement the diverse views presented in this chapter.

Spencer E. Ante	"Keeping Out the Wrong People," *Business Week*, October 4, 2004.
Fred Barnes	"Bordering on a Victory," *Weekly Standard*, April 24, 2006.
Jennifer Bennett	"Operation Return to Sender," May 30, 2008. www.slate.com.
The Economist	"Decapitating the Snakeheads," October 8, 2005.
Michael Elliott	"Why So Many French Voted for a Bigot," *Time*, May 6, 2002.
Harlan Koff	"Security, Markets and Power: The Relationship Between EU Enlargement and Immigration," *Journal of European Integration*, December 2005.
Stanley Kurtz	"Immigration Crackdown," *National Review*, June 25, 2007.
Robert S. Leiken	"Europe's Angry Muslims," *Foreign Affairs*, July 2005.
Alexander Moens and Martin Collacott	"Immigration, National Security and Canadian-American Relations," *Fraser Forum*, December 2007.
James Slack	"Immigration: The Biggest Problem Our Country Faces," *The Express*, January 11, 2005.
Tom Tancredo	"Immigration, Citizenship, and National Security: The Silent Invasion," *Mediterranean Quarterly*, Fall 2004.
Jan C. Ting	"Immigration and National Security," *Orbis*, January 2006.

For Further Discussion

Chapter 1

1. Per Gustafson describes the main reasons that Sweden has changed its citizenship laws to make it easier for immigrants to acquire political and social rights. Do you agree with his rationale for the changes? Should the new policies be adopted by other countries?

2. Based on Zygmunt Dzieciolowski's viewpoint, why does Russia need to reform its immigration laws? Meanwhile, Edwige Liliane LeFebvre criticizes France's immigration laws. Are his criticisms of France similar to those Dzieciolowski has of Russia? What are the main differences or similarities?

3. Souheila Al-Jadda is very critical of the way the United States treats legal immigrants. Would the reforms discussed in the viewpoint fix the delays and other problems the viewpoint cites?

Chapter 2

1. Piaras MacÉinrí and Paddy Walley's viewpoint was originally published by the Immigrant Council of Ireland, an organization that advocates on behalf of immigrant rights. Is there a bias in their viewpoint, or have they presented both sides in a fair and balanced fashion?

2. Tony McNicol argues that Japan needs more immigrants to maintain the country's economy. Does the author make a good argument? What are the main weaknesses in the viewpoint?

3. What are the main reasons that Shunil Roy-Chaudhuri believes that Great Britain needs more immigrants? What are the primary ways in which immigrants help the British

economy? Why don't many people in Britain recognize these benefits, according to the viewpoint?

Chapter 3

1. According to Amitai Etzioni, immigrants have both rights and responsibilities. What does he list as the most important responsibilities that immigrants have when they come to a new country? Do you agree with his contentions?

2. Graeme Hamilton discusses efforts by local communities to prompt immigrants to adhere to the dominant customs and social conventions of the area. Is it appropriate for communities to force newcomers to integrate into the mainstream?

3. Jonathan Kandell argues that American expatriates have had a major influence in the Czech capital of Prague. What are the main examples that Kandell cites in the viewpoint to support his points?

Chapter 4

1. Adnan Khan asserts that Canada's current immigration laws do not effectively protect the country from the threat of terrorism. Do you agree with his main points? Why or why not?

2. According to the viewpoint by Stephen de Tarczynski, why did Australia change its immigration laws? What were the most controversial aspects of the previous policy? Should the old laws have been changed?

3. How have Chinese immigrants negatively impacted the border region between China and Russia, according to Mikhail A. Alexseev and C. Richard Hofstetter. Do the authors provide compelling evidence to support their main points?

Organizations to Contact

The editors have compiled the following list of organizations concerned with the issues debated in this book. The descriptions are derived from materials provided by the organizations. All have publications or information available for interested readers. The list was compiled on the date of publication of the present volume; the information provided here may change. Be aware that many organizations take several weeks or longer to respond to inquiries, so allow as much time as possible.

American Enterprise Institute
1150 Seventeenth Street NW, Washington, DC   20036
(202) 862-5800 • Fax: (202) 862-7177
E-mail: NRI@aei.org
Web site: www.aei.org

The American Enterprise Institute (AEI) is a nonprofit, non-partisan organization that advocates limited government and private-enterprise solutions to public policy issues. AEI was founded in 1943 and is one of the more prestigious conservative think tanks. AEI opposes open immigration and has called for both reforms and better enforcement of existing immigration measures.

Brookings Institute
1775 Massachusetts Avenue NW, Washington, DC   20036
(202) 797 6000 • Fax: (202) 536 3623
E-mail: communications@brookings.edu
Web site: www.brookings.edu

The Brookings Institute is a nonprofit, independent research organization in Washington, D.C. It was founded in 1927. The Brookings Institute sponsors research and dialogue on a range of domestic and international issues. The organization supports expanded rights for immigrants and immigration reform in the United States.

Bruegel
33 Rue de la Charité/Liefdadigheidsstraat 33
Brussels   B-1210
  Belgium
32 2 227 4210 • Fax: 32 2 227 4219
E-mail: info@bruegel.org
Web site: www.bruegel.org

Bruegel, also known as the Brussels European and Global Economic Laboratory, is a research organization funded by the European Union (EU). Bruegel was founded in 2002 and named in honor of Pieter Bruegel, a sixteenth-century Flemish painter known for innovation. Bruegel conducts research on issues such as immigration for the EU.

Carnegie Endowment for International Peace
1779 Massachusetts Avenue NW, Washington, DC   20036
(202) 483 7600 • Fax (202) 483 1840
E-mail: info@ceip.org
Web site: www.carnegieendowment.org

The Carnegie Endowment for International Peace is an American nonprofit research organization that promotes scholarship on globalization and international security and trade, including studies of human migration. Founded in 1910, the endowment promotes international peace and stability. It publishes the highly regarded journal, *Foreign Policy*.

Cato Institute
1000 Massachusetts Avenue NW, Washington, DC   20001
(202) 842-0200 • Fax: (202) 842 3490
e-mail: pr@cato.org
Web site: www.cato.org

The Cato Institute, an American nonprofit, libertarian public-policy research center, was founded in 1977 by Edward H. Crane. The institute promotes limited government, free enterprise and individual choice. The Cato Institute sponsors seminars and conferences on public policy and it publishes a variety of materials, many of which are available on its Web site. It supports immigration reform in the United States.

Center for Immigration Studies
1522 K Street NW, Suite 820, Washington, DC   20005-1202
(202) 466-8185 • Fax: (202) 466-8076
E-mail: center@cis.org
Web site: www.cis.org

The Center for Immigration Studies is an independent, non-profit organization that advocates low immigration and increased border security to reduce illegal immigration. Founded in 1985, the conservative Center produces a number of publications on immigration policy and lobbies the government to enact more restrictive immigration laws. Its Web site has a section where the public can post immigration questions for the Center's experts to answer.

The Center for Strategic and International Studies
1800 K Street NW, Washington, DC   20006
(202) 887-0200 • Fax: (202) 775-3199
E-mail: aschwartz@csis.org
Web site: www.csis.org

The Center for Strategic and International Studies (CSIS) is a nonpartisan research organization. CSIS was founded in 1962 and has grown to be one of the world's largest public policy think tanks. Its scholars and researchers cover all areas of the world and all major topics in international relations, including immigration. CSIS publishes the journal *Washington Quarterly*.

Council on Foreign Relations
1779 Massachusetts Avenue NW
Washington, DC   20036-2103
(202) 483 7600 • Fax: (202) 483 1840
E-mail: info@CarnegieEndowment.org
Web site: www.cfr.org

The Council on Foreign Relations (CFR) was formed in 1921. CFR is a nonpartisan, nonprofit research organization. Its mission is to be a resource on foreign policy issues for business, government, and the public. The CFR produces a range of reports, studies, and books. It also publishes the journal *Foreign Affairs.* The CFR has issued a number of publications on immigration.

Immigrant Council of Ireland
2 St. Andrew Street, Dublin 2
  Ireland
(01) 674 0200 • Fax: (01) 645 8059
E-mail: info@immigrantcouncil.ie
Web site: www.immigrantcouncil.ie

Founded in 2001, the Immigrant Council of Ireland is an independent, nongovernmental organization that advocates on behalf of migrant rights. The council sponsors research on immigration and works to enact laws that protect migrants. It conducts training programs for businesses and local governments on immigrant rights. The council also has a law center that represents immigrants.

Joint Council for the Welfare of Immigrants
115 Old Street, London   EC1V 9RT
  United Kingdom
+44 02 (0) 7251 8708 • Fax: +44 02 (0) 7251 8707
E-mail: info@jcwi.org.uk
Web site: www.jcwi.org.uk

The Joint Council for the Welfare of Immigrants is a private volunteer organization that was formed in the United Kingdom in 1967 to counter racism and anti-immigrant sentiment. The council provides legal assistance for immigrants and offers training to companies and other bodies on immigrant rights. The Council also produces studies and other publications on immigration policy.

National Council of La Raza
Raul Yzaguirre Building, 1126 Sixteenth Street NW
Washington, DC   20036
(202) 785-1670 • Fax: (202) 776-1792
E-mail: comments@nclr.org
Web site: www.nclr.org

The National Council of La Raza is a Hispanic advocacy group in the United States with eight regional offices and more than 300 local chapters or affiliated groups in forty-one states. Founded in 1968, the group has been a staunch proponent of open immigration. It has also worked to improve immigrant rights. La Raza publishes a range of studies and position papers on issues of concern to Hispanics, and sponsors a number of public events each year.

Open Europe
7 Tufton Street, London   SW1P 3QN
   United Kingdom
0207 197 2333 • Fax: 0207 197 2307
E-mail: info@openeurope.org.uk
Web site: www.openeurope.org.uk

Open Europe is a British advocacy group that supports deep reforms for the European Union (EU), including revisions to the EU's migration policies. Open Europe was established by business leaders in the United Kingdom and the organization supports conservative, free-market solutions to societal problems and argues for more local control over issues such as immigration.

Bibliography of Books

Aderanti Adepoju, Ton van Naerssen, and Annelies Zoomers, eds. *International Migration and National Development in Sub-Saharan Africa.* Boston, MA: Brill, 2008.

Greg Anrig Jr. and Tova Andrea Wang, eds. *Immigration's New Frontiers: Experiences from the Emerging Gateway States.* New York, NY: Century Foundation Press, 2006.

Elliot R. Barkan, ed. *Immigration, Incorporation and Transnationalism.* New Brunswick, NJ: Transaction Publishers, 2007.

Bruce Bawer. *While Europe Slept: How Islam Is Destroying the West from Within.* New York, NY: Doubleday, 2006.

Didier Bigo and Elspeth Guild. *Controlling Frontiers: Free Movement into and Within Europe.* Aldershot, UK: Ashgate, 2005.

John Biles, Meyer Burstein, and James Frideres, eds. *Immigration and Integration in Canada in the Twenty-First Century.* Kingston, Ont.: Queen's University, 2008.

David C. Brotherton and Philip Kretsedemas, eds. *Keeping Out the Other: A Critical Introduction to Immigration Enforcement Today.* New York, NY: Columbia University Press, 2008.

Mirjam De Bruijn, Rijk Van Dijk, and Dick Foeken, eds. *Mobile Africa: Changing Patterns of Movement in Africa and Beyond.* Boston, MA: Brill, 2001.

Jorge G. Castaneda — *Ex Mex: From Migrants to Immigrants.* New York, NY: Norton, 2007.

Mark I. Choate — *Emigrant Nation: The Making of Italy Abroad.* Cambridge, MA: Harvard University Press, 2008.

Michael Dummett — *On Immigration and Refugees.* New York, NY: Routledge, 2001.

Bill Edgar, Joe Doherty and Henk Meert — *Immigration and Homelessness in Europe.* Bristol, UK: Policy Press, 2004.

Thierry Fabre and Paul Sant-Cassia — *Between Europe and the Mediterranean: The Challenges and the Fears.* New York, NY: Palgrave, 2007.

Thomas Faist and Andreas Ette, eds. — *The Europeanization of National Policies and Politics of Immigration: Between Autonomy and the European Union.* New York, NY: Palgrave Macmillan, 2007.

Bryan Fanning, ed. — *Immigration and Social Change in the Republic of Ireland.* New York, NY: Palgrave, 2007.

Mary Foner — *In a New Land: A Comparative View of Immigration.* New York, NY: New York University Press, 2005.

Jane Freedman — *Immigration and Insecurity in France.* Aldershot, UK: Ashgate, 2004.

Holger Henke — *Crossing Over: Comparing Recent Migration in the United States and Europe.* Lanham, MD: Lexington Books, 2005.

Michel Korinman and John Laughland, eds. *The Long March to the West: Twenty-First Century Migration in Europe and the Greater Mediterranean Area.* Edgware, UK: Vallentine Mitchell, 2007.

Philip A. Kuhn *Chinese Among Others: Emigration in Modern Times.* Lanham, MD: Rowman & Littlefield, 2008.

Paul McCaffrey, ed. *Hispanic Americans.* New York, NY: H. W. Wilson, 2007.

Anthony M. Messina and Gallya Lahay *The Migration Reader: Exploring Politics and Policies.* Boulder, CO: Lynne Rienner, 2006.

Jonathan W. Moses *International Migration: Globalization's Last Frontier.* New York, NY: Palgrave, 2006.

Sonia Nazario *Enrique's Journey.* New York, NY: Random House, 2006.

Margaret Sands Orchowski *Immigration and the American Dream: Battling the Political Hype and Hysteria.* Lanham, MD: Rowman & Littlefield, 2008.

Demetrios G. Papademetriou *Europe and Its Immigrants in the 21st Century: A New Deal of a Continuing Dialogue of the Deaf.* Washington, DC: Migration Policy Institute, 2006.

Andres Schloenhardt *Migrant Smuggling: Illegal Migration and Organised Crime in Australia and the Asia Pacific.* Herndon, VA: Brill, 2003.

W. M. Spellman — *Uncertain Identity: International Migration Since 1945.* London, UK: Reaktion Books, 2008.

Will Summerville — *Immigration Under New Labour.* Bristol, UK: Policy Press, 2007.

Dominic Thomas — *Black France: Colonialism, Immigration and Transnationalism.* Bloomington, IN: Indiana University press, 2007.

Jeffrey M. Togman — *The Ramparts of Nations: Institutions and Immigration Policies in France and the United States.* Westport, CT: Praeger, 2002.

Index

Geographic headings and page numbers in **boldface** refer to viewpoints about that country or region.